Follow
the St★r

Presented to the
Clayton Community Library
by

CLAYTON BUSINESS

&

COMMUNITY ASSOCIATION

Also by T. D. Jakes
in Large Print:

Cover Girls
God's Leading Lady

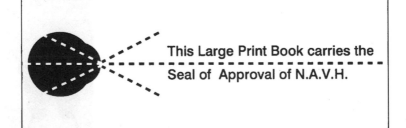

This Large Print Book carries the
Seal of Approval of N.A.V.H.

Follow the St★r

Christmas Stories
That Changed My Life

T. D. Jakes

Published in 2004 by arrangement with G. P. Putnam's Sons, a division of Penguin Group (USA) Inc.

The text of this Large Print edition is unabridged. Other aspects of the book may vary from the original edition.

Set in 16 pt. Plantin by Al Chase.

Printed in the United States on permanent paper.

The Library of Congress has cataloged the Thorndike Press® edition as follows:

Jakes, T. D.
    Follow the star : Christmas stories that changed my life / T.D. Jakes. — Large print ed.
        p. cm. — (Thorndike Press large print Christian living)
    ISBN 0-7862-6614-7 (lg. print : hc : alk. paper)
    ISBN 1-59415-044-3 (lg. print : sc : alk. paper)
    1. Christmas.   I. Title.   II. Thorndike Press large print Christian living series.
GT4985.J34 2004
394.2663—dc22   2004006331

Follow
the St★r

As the Founder/CEO of NAVH, the only national health agency solely devoted to those who, although not totally blind, have an eye disease which could lead to serious visual impairment, I am pleased to recognize Thorndike Press★ as one of the leading publishers in the large print field.

Founded in 1954 in San Francisco to prepare large print textbooks for partially seeing children, NAVH became the pioneer and standard setting agency in the preparation of large type.

Today, those publishers who meet our standards carry the prestigious "Seal of Approval" indicating high quality large print. We are delighted that Thorndike Press is one of the publishers whose titles meet these standards. We are also pleased to recognize the significant contribution Thorndike Press is making in this important and growing field.

Lorraine H. Marchi, L.H.D.
Founder/CEO
NAVH

★ Thorndike Press encompasses the following imprints: Thorndike, Wheeler, Walker and Large Print Press.

Acknowledgments

My gratitude to my wife, Serita, and my entire family, who generously shared me with this manuscript. Thank you for being such a blessed gift in my life everyday. I also want to acknowledge the compassion and encouragement that I consistently receive from my church family.

Thank you, Denise Silvestro, for your insights and creativity, and for working tirelessly to bring my message to fruition.

Thank you, Joel Fotinos, for your enthusiasm, encouragement, wisdom, and for continuing to believe in me.

Thank you to everyone at Putnam. You always treat me and my work with great dignity and integrity. My gratitude to Susan Petersen Kennedy, Marilyn Ducksworth, Dan Harvey, Dick Heffernan, Chris Mosley, Martha Bushko, Meredith Phebus, Timothy Meyer, and everyone at JMS Marketing and Sales, Inc.

Thank you, Tom Winters, for your wise counsel. And to Beth Clark, whose skills helped make *Follow the Star* possible.

Contents

Introduction

Billions of them dance across the night sky — diamonds in the darkness, points of light against a canopy of endless black. They have shone for ages and ages, lending their glow to the night for millions of years. Venture outside the city, away from the street lamps and neon signs shining in shop windows downtown, away from the pollution, and look up. They will shimmer and glimmer as if they've been freshly hurled across that dark expanse by the hand of God Himself.

They are the stars — most of them nameless, few of them ever noteworthy on their own. Except one. In the history of the universe, one star outshines the rest. That star made a statement. That was the star that heralded hope for all who would ever gaze heavenward again.

Perhaps it began as an ordinary star and grew brighter and brighter until all others seemed dim. Or perhaps it burst against an ebony backdrop like a flashbulb in a dark room. Whatever the case, it hung like God's favorite ornament in the sky that night and it commanded the attention of the mere mortals below.

I could write the story myself, in my own words, but I could never express it as dignified and grandly as Matthew did in the Gospel that bears his name.

Now after Jesus was born in Bethlehem of Judea in the days of Herod the king, behold, wise men from the East came to Jerusalem, saying, "Where is He who has been born King of the Jews? For we have seen His star in the East and have come to worship Him." . . . And he sent them to Bethlehem and said, "Go and search carefully for the young Child, and when you have found Him, bring back word to me, that I may come and worship Him also." When they heard the king, they departed; and behold, the star which they had seen in the East went before them, till it came and stood over where the young Child was. When they saw the star, they rejoiced with exceedingly great joy.
MATTHEW 2:1–2; 8–10

This star called the wise men to worship and caused them to rejoice. But it was

14

nothing more than a light for their pilgrim path. It was not the object of their worship; it simply pointed the way. And when it stopped, when at last it stood still in the sky, they knew they had arrived at their destination and their journey had ended.

But it had really just begun.

There in the stable under the star, those wise men first laid human eyes on holy flesh. They encountered God on earth. They must have known in their hearts the magnitude of the moment. When they entered the place where the little Boy lay, they fell down and worshiped Him. I wonder how long it took for them to compose themselves in the presence of such greatness, even though His majesty was small enough to hold in one hand.

The radiant star they had followed as they traveled to see Him must have vanished from their memories when they looked into the tiny face in the manger. In fact, in this story of the Savior's birth, there really is only one Star — and His name is Jesus. I believe that He is the Star of the great drama called history. I believe that, without Him, life is missing its focal point. Without Him, the paths we travel on during our years here are rocky and slippery, our days are dark and empty. He is not only the One we worship; He is the One we follow. He is the only One we can trust to lead us, the only One worth walking behind.

I have walked behind this Star for years, following Him day by day on the most adventurous and amazing journey. This Christmas, I would like to share with you some of the stories from a lifetime spent following Him. So I hope you'll make yourself a cup of hot chocolate and curl up by the fire. Take time to enjoy one man's Christmas memories and make some of your own. And in the midst of the hustle and the bustle and the hurry of the season, don't forget to look up — and follow the Star.

1

Life Is a Journey

We were five passengers making our Christmastime road trip in a fume-filled, rust-covered, partially broken rendition of a family car. My parents bounced along the highway on the front seat, while all three children — my brother, my sister, and I — were piled up in the back, wrestling and tussling, giggling and complaining. The laughter and teasing was always interrupted by someone's squealing and the clamor always reached its high point when my brother pinched my sister and I, the baby of the family, began to whine because I was hungry.

The West Virginia mountains through which we drove were beautiful but often perilous. With my nose pressed against the car window (during those rare moments when I did not have to sit in the middle of the backseat), I saw the winding roads, laced with snow and sleet, and ice hanging from mountain peaks like stalactites in a cave. It looked like a winter wonderland. But while the beauty awed my mother, the clutter of cars and the twists in the road aggravated my father. The traffic and difficult driving conditions were enough to drive a sane man to the edge of exasperation.

Together, my mother and father played a symphony of diverse moods and attitudes and comments that soared toward a crescendo as the journey continued — if you know what I mean. How well I recall those memorable experiences when we were all there on the highway, trying to get to our destination and trapped in traffic. Even worse, we were usually in a hurry and did not have much gas. Add to that the fact that my father had a tendency to get lost and would rather have danced naked in a roaring fire than admit it. And to top it off, my precious mother, God rest her soul, had a nasty habit of informing him that he was lost. Ah yes, it was always quite a trip.

If my father had only consulted a map, we would have been able to get where we were going with much less angst. But left to his instincts (and his unwillingness to ask for directions), we often ended up traveling away from our goal instead of toward it! What started out as a pleasant trip soon ended up wrought with stress and tensions as time passed and the place we were trying to reach eluded us. As I remember, usually just about the time the harsh reality that we were not accomplishing our goal set in, I had to — well, you know — I had to *go;* and that didn't help the situation at all!

Holidays should be a joyful time and family outings should be fun, but when you are trying to get somewhere in a hurry on a slick road, surrounded by many drivers, the trip can be quite stressful. My parents were not alone in their longing for holiday happiness. Millions of other people were seeking it too. (I know because we saw them on the highway!) Some were singing Christmas carols and some were sullen. Some were sober and some were not. Some, like we, were rushing to their destination so that when they arrived, they could turn around and rush home.

At any point along the way, my father could have looked at a map or done what he inevitably did, which was to finally ask someone at a gas station, "Is this the road to [wherever]? How much farther do we need to go to get there?" He could have done that, but he rarely did — not until tempers were flaring, frustrations were mounting, and patience was wearing thin.

Now that I am grown and have children of my own, I see that, like my childhood car trips, life is really just a journey too. I find myself wanting to veer off of the mangled, tangled traffic jam called life, stop at a spiritual gas station, and echo my father's questions: "How far do I have to go to get there? Am I on the right road? Shouldn't I have been farther than I am now?" I could go on and on and on; I have a thousand questions to ask the Lord about the journey.

A person really doesn't have to live too long to realize that life is a journey. Along our way, we often find that the weather can be inclement and the conditions around us unfavorable. At times, the hustle and bustle can be overwhelming, and the noises of daily living can drown out our own thoughts. Somebody's radio is blasting, horns are honking, and people are traveling in all modes of transportation in every direction with every conceivable expression on their faces. Like the twisted highways of many large metropolises, life is filled with exit ramps and entrance ramps, merging traffic, and cautions. If that is not enough, there are the dangerous accidents, slick spots, and incessant road-rage drivers who make the journey even more perilous. It also seems like everyone is speeding, so we have to go faster and faster just to keep from getting run over! The worst part is that the clock is ticking while we journey, and we are in a race where every second counts. We have only a certain amount of time to reach our destination, and each day we live is a day we will never see again.

Given the choice, I think many of us would park our vehicles under a nice shade tree at a rest stop, if that were possible, and avoid the chaos all together. You know as well as I do that, in reality, we do not have the option to withdraw from the rat race. Like it or not, as long as we live, we find ourselves seemingly predestined to travel somewhere. Some will go forward, some will be stuck in reverse, and some will seem to go around and around and around like a little puppy chasing his tail.

But unlike a road trip, life's journey does not come with explicit directions of which way to go, when to turn, and how long it will take us to get there. It does not even come with a globe that will allow us to see the big picture! All of us do not have the same purposes and the same goals. While we want to go to heaven, ultimately, we will spend our time on this earth in as many different ways as there are stars in the sky. Some will marry and some will stay single all of their lives. Some will raise children and some will not. Some will enter into ministry and some will pursue other careers. Some will work from the left side of their brain and some from the right. Some will educate themselves and some will excel in other arenas. Some will travel the same highway for a season but take different exits. Yes, we are all on the journey, but each of us has his own course to run.

The apostle Paul said to Timothy, "I have finished my course," and that must be your focus too. To finish the course set before you — not your father's course, not your best friend's course, not anybody else's course, but *yours*.

I think I know what you'd like to ask. You may be wondering how you can find your way through the maze of life and keep moving toward your purpose? The answer is actually quite simple, and it is the same for all of us. We have to follow our Guide, like the wise men did in ancient days as they pursued the Baby Jesus. We simply have to follow the Star.

Where is the Star? Oh, it is not in the sky as it was for them. The Star we follow is Jesus, and if we let Him, He will live inside of us and guide us toward our destination.

There is no getting off the road of life and asking for directions. You can ask directions from your minister or spiritual advisor. You can consult the only map we have and the only one we need — the Word of the Lord. But the best compass you have is the Spirit that dwells within you. It will get you through the traffic, teach you when to merge, advise you of your speed, and get you to the right place at the right time. Even though our family trips were often longer than they needed to be, more stressful than was necessary, and a bit grating on the nerves, I simply cannot remember a single time when we didn't get where we were trying to go! And the same is true for your life. My prayer for you is that you would know in your heart, be at rest in your mind, and get settled in your spirit, that God knows exactly how to get you there too — wherever your "there" is.

This holiday season is just one stop on a long journey toward an undisclosed destination. Much of what you will face in your life is currently hidden from your view. No mirrors, windshields, or navigational devices will let you see everything that awaits you ahead. But remember that as you travel, if you have a little faith in the trunk and a little gas in the tank, you will eventually get there. I'd be willing to bet that you'll like what you see when you arrive.

Just one more word: Enjoy those whom God has given you to accompany you on the journey of your life. Families are never perfect, and if you could ask my parents, they would tell you that families are full of challenges and aggravations. But you know what? The people with whom we share childhood memories, DNA, and a last name are a real blessing. Take courage, fill up your tank, drive forward, and enjoy the trip. You are on the ride of a lifetime. When in doubt, look up; when troubled, look within; and when in darkness, always, always follow the Star.

May your happy holidays begin right now.

2

Come, Ye Thankful People

There are certain holidays people cannot ignore, and Christmas is one of them. Retailers clamor for our attention with signs and banners and decorations more extravagant than ever before. Office parties and open houses kick into full swing, while children nearly burst with excitement over their upcoming holidays. Fast-food restaurants replace their paper goods with holiday-themed napkins and cups, and some people even put wreaths on their cars. Inevitably, a woman sporting Christmas ornament earrings (or a man with a tie that plays "Jingle Bells") will show up in your field of vision. On top of all that, even if you wanted to take a break and lose yourself in your regular television schedule, you couldn't — because most of the shows are preempted by holiday movies and specials! And then, of course, to be downright practical, if you checked your calendar you would see "Christmas Day" printed on the page or the square for December 25.

See what I mean? Whether or not a person celebrates Christmas, its existence is undeniable.

Thanksgiving, on the other hand, could almost slide by with hardly a mention. It could just fall right off the calendar and some people would barely notice. Now, I realize that part of the issue with Thanksgiving is that it does not occur on the same day every year. At the same time, though, our commercial culture garners little profit from that particular holiday, so it gets less public hype. Level with me: have *you* ever gotten a Thanksgiving present? Oh, I know that turkey sales peak at Thanksgiving. No doubt sweet potato revenues increase; green beans and ready-made graham cracker crusts probably end up in the black as well. But beyond the grocery stores, nobody really benefits from Thanksgiving financially except maybe some florists or other little gift shops that sell fall decorations.

On second thought, someone does benefit from Thanksgiving: you. You do, and I do, and so do a whole host of praising people who know the value and the power of gratitude. For starters, gratitude reminds us that we are not self-sufficient. Being thankful shifts our focus away from our needs and onto our blessings; it turns our hearts away from ourselves and onto the Lord, Who is the Giver of every good and perfect gift. I tell you that He is the source of every blessing, large and small. All good things come to us from His hand — the beauty of a sunrise, the discipline of a job to do, the joy of having a friend. I could write all day about His goodness, but I suspect you have your very own list of benefits. The Bible says that He gives us all things richly to enjoy, and being thankful causes the demons of lack to flee and praise to spring forth from the core of our being.

Expressing our gratitude also keeps us humble. It's hard to be proud when you are thanking God from a place of sincerity. Oh yes, it is difficult indeed to be arrogant or haughty when you are praising Him for rescuing you from a desperate situation or for working a miracle in your life. When He does for you what you cannot do for yourself — and what no other human being is able to do for you — well, that kind of love provokes a response of truly humble thanksgiving. Because God is so good, humility has its own blessings. For instance, the Bible says, in several places, that God resists the proud or the scornful but that He gives grace to the humble. Now I don't know about you, but I cannot imagine anyone not needing all the grace they can get!

But like humility, the giving of thanks doesn't always come naturally. Sometimes we have to pinch ourselves and be reminded to be thankful. We have to be mindful of our expressions of gratitude, just as we have to be mindful of the observance of Thanksgiving Day. We have to make an effort to stay grounded in gratitude so that the swirl of Christmas preparations will not pick us up and carry us away! I even know people who will not think of beginning to decorate for Christmas before Thanksgiving because they are so determined that they and their loved ones are going to stop on that day and at the very least, breathe a grateful prayer.

Our family has always been that way. For years, we went to church on Thanksgiving morning, choosing to give God His praise before we went home to stuff ourselves with turkey and dressing and cranberry sauce and sweet potato pie. There was something so special about those services — special enough that the church members were willing to excuse themselves from holiday visitors and press through the peer pressure of hungry families and gather in the sanctuary for a few glorious moments. I can still see the bright, smiling faces of the men and women, boys and girls who joined together to celebrate God's goodness on those cool, crisp mornings, when a few remaining fall leaves clung to the tree branches and caused the West Virginia mountains to glow like the embers of a bonfire. When it came to material possessions, we did not have as much as some people, but oh my, were we ever blessed! When we sang God's praises, they bellowed from the bottom of our hearts, and when we said, "Thank You, Lord!" we meant it with every fiber of our beings.

Because life can be difficult for all of us at times, you may be weathering your own personal storms right now. Perhaps there is a trouble in your family, or maybe you are in such internal conflict that the turmoil is churning within your very soul. Can I tell you something that will help you? Praise through the pain. Determine that you will not be silent and that there is no circumstance on earth mighty enough to keep you from praising your Father. If you struggle at first, look for the small, everyday blessings. You may even need to start by being thankful that you are alive and well enough to face your problem!

Whatever you are going through, contend for your own thanksgiving. Make up your mind that you are going to thank God in every circumstance and crush the devil with the power of your praise. Did you catch that? I slipped a Bible verse in on you when I wrote to "thank God in every circumstance." Now the Bible doesn't say that you must give thanks *for* everything, but it does say "*in* everything give thanks" (1 Thessalonians 5:18, italics mine). Just in case you try to find a loophole, the apostle Paul then writes, "For this is the will of God in Christ Jesus for you." That leaves no room for lack of gratitude! If you want to know God's will, start here. Start by giving thanks in everything.

There is a certain kind of strength that comes from praising God, and there is a more vigorous strength that comes from praising Him when your life is not running as smoothly as you would like. I believe our ability to thank Him and to praise Him corresponds to the depth of our intimacy with Him and our loving trust in Him. For example, when you know that He is your provider, you will be able to thank Him when a pink slip shows up in your in-box. When you know how much He loves you, you will be able to thank Him when your boyfriend decides to end your relationship. (Come on, when you know how much He loves you, you may decide to end the relationship yourself!) You will so completely trust His heart toward you and His plans for you that you will be utterly confident in His goodness and nothing can cause you to waver.

When we speak of "the holiday season," we are really talking about that period of five weeks or so that begins with Thanksgiving Day and ends on New Year's. We start the holidays with turkey and dressing and finish it with black-eyed peas! As we move from late November into December and then on to January 1, we quickly lose our grateful focus on the goodness of the Lord and, instead, begin to concentrate on everything from filling stockings to buying a new calendar. I think the holiday schedule is really brilliant, though, because it starts off with the right emphasis: a thankful heart.

I believe we need to begin to stay thankful, not just through the holiday season, but all year long. Yes, we need to live in a constant state of Thanksgiving. Honestly, thanksgiving should become a way of life and not just a code word for the year's best meal. Let's decide now that Thanksgiving will no longer be simply a prelude to Christmas but a continuation of our loving appreciation of God's goodness to us. As I think about this holiday season, I've realized that perhaps the key to a really great Christmas is a never-ending Thanksgiving. And that's what I wish for you.

3

Exceedingly Abundantly

I was about eleven years old when my eyes first caught a glimpse of the old upright piano through the big window of the Arbogast Piano store on MacCorkle Avenue in South Charleston, West Virginia. I walked into the store, with enthusiasm and caution battling for dominance in my young mind, and I approached it as timidly as a little boy who had finally gotten the nerve to talk to that cute little girl on the playground. It was *exactly* what I wanted. I could hardly wait to take my mother to see it. The first chance I got, I convinced her to accompany me downtown to behold for herself the object of my young heart's desire.

That time, I marched up to it as if it were already mine and presented it to my mother. Running my hand over its cabinet as tenderly as I would stroke the fur of an ailing pet, we stood in the store and admired the piano together. After a few seconds of appropriate awe, I pleaded with her, "This one would be very good. This one would be just perfect for me."

My mother was part Blackfoot Indian, and she had that Indian ability to show absolutely no emotion in certain situations. There was no way to read what she was thinking, and her only response to me regarding the piano was, "Well, we'll see." Looking back, I now know that she was genuinely delighted by my desire for a piano, but she veiled her excitement like a professional actress. She never *promised* us anything, preferring to keep us in suspense and to make sure we had just enough doubt so that when we got whatever we were longing for, we would be shocked and surprised. Watching our reactions tickled and thrilled her as much as the gifts tickled and thrilled us!

It wasn't a new piano; it was, as we say today, "previously owned." But I did not care, it was still a piano, and that was good enough for me. I could play only three songs. Well, almost three — I could only play one hand of the third one so far. *But,* I thought, *Soon. I know I can play that song soon if I just had something to practice on.* I didn't mind practicing; in fact, I was eager to practice because I wanted so desperately to play. After I knew three songs, then I would learn a fourth; then there would be five. Before you knew it, I would have a repertoire to rival any in town! Of course I would!

I had fallen in love with music. I can't really explain it to you, but there always seemed to be a song inside of me. There has been a beat in my blood and a melody in my mind for as long as I can remember. Just as I knew there was music within me, I also *knew* I was going to get a piano someday. I did not assume that I would get the one I had chosen, but I thought I would. After all, I was the baby of the family, and I usually ended up getting what I wanted. Somehow, some way — I just knew it. I was well aware that the price of a new piano far exceeded what we could afford, and I knew much better than to expect one. But the used one was within our reach — if we stretched our money really, really far.

I wanted it so bad. "I can make do with this one," I declared to my mother, "I really can."

I had her wrapped around my little finger. But I knew that buying a piano was not an everyday occurrence. No, a purchase of that magnitude was reserved for a special occasion — say, for instance, a birthday. Or better yet, Christmas.

My hopes for a piano were high when I

awoke that Christmas morning. Jumping out of bed, I made a beeline for the stairs but stopped dead in my tracks when I heard my sister's skilled fingers tickling an ivory keyboard. Then my feet could not run fast enough! I thought I would fall right down the staircase trying to get there to see it, to hear it, to squeal with glee.

It was not the dark brown, heavily lacquered piano I had chosen.

No, it certainly was not the one I had picked out. But there it was, as big as life — a *brand-new* piano. It took my breath away.

"Look!" I cried, rubbing my eyes in disbelief. "Wow! Look at this piano!"

It was so nice, a real beauty — a rich, mahogany piano with an elegant sheen, dressed in a bright red bow. It still smelled new. It was much too big to put under the tree, but it was my Christmas present — all mine.

Even as it stood proudly on its gleaming legs in the middle of our living room, I could hardly believe it was actually in our house. It was right in front of my face, where I could see it, but I couldn't believe it. It was one of the best Christmas experiences of my entire life.

Heaven only knows what all my mother sacrificed in order to get that new piano.

But I know now that she realized that I would not give up on my dream of playing the piano, even though I had only mastered three songs (okay, two and a half). She had observed me, as only a mother can, and she knew my character — that I was diligent, that I had what it took to "stick to it," and that if I had made up my mind to play the piano, then I would play the piano.

Coupled with my commitment to make music, I had a mother who continually stoked the fires of my dreams by listening as I spoke of them, by taking me seriously, and by asking me questions that would cause me to think in ways that would help me pull my dreams out of make-believe and into reality. On top of that, she did absolutely everything within her power to provide me with the tools and resources and support I needed to pursue the dreams I carried. That wonderful lady really believed I could do anything I wanted to if I worked hard enough. And because she believed it, I grew up believing it too.

Most of all, though, my mother wanted me to have the best. And something about having the best challenged me to do my best. She recognized my love for music and rewarded my diligence. She listened as I shared my dream of playing the piano and responded without saying a word. By buying me that new piano, she told me, "All right then. You want to play the piano? Then you are going to have one fine piano." She was not willing to let me settle for somebody else's piano. No, she was determined to dignify my dream with a brand-new, beautiful piano. It was her way of shouting, "You can do it! You've got what it takes to play this exquisite instrument! Now go for it!"

I loved that piano and, just as we knew I would, I practiced with dedication and I ended up being able to play well — if I do say so myself! Through the years, the piano was a companion to me, and it was the instrument that allowed me to express myself on countless occasions. Believe it or not, that piano was the same one I used when I opened my first church years later, and it was the same piano I used when I started my ministry. It was there when I began to preach, and it was there as I built the foundation of all that I am doing today. It really was the gift that keeps on giving!

That story reminds me of a verse in the Bible. There are lots of ways to encounter the truths of God's word and have them spring to life inside your very being, and sometimes we learn their truth before we ever learn their words. And that is what happened to me when I received the brand-new piano. As a boy, I would never have given these words to my experience with the piano, but I understood their truth in a way no preacher or Sunday school teacher could have ever imparted. Here they are: "Now to Him who is able to do exceedingly abundantly above all that we ask or think, according to the power that works in us, to Him be glory in the church by Christ Jesus to all generations, forever and ever. Amen" (Ephesians 3:20–21).

I want you to know that God is able to do exceedingly abundantly above all that you could ever ask or think. Please, don't just read these words with your eyes or try to understand with your mind but allow them to soak into your soul. This is *you* we are talking about. Yes, you. God is not only able to do more than you would dare request. He *wants* to do exceedingly abundantly more than you can ever imagine. I wanted desperately to play the piano, and I asked for a used instrument on which to practice. But God saw to it that I received more than I ever thought I could receive. That gift exceeded all my expectations, and my dreams were fulfilled far beyond learning to play that third song.

As for the piano that greeted me that Christmas morning, it was played often and treasured through the years. It is gone now, but the love remains. I am as confident and secure in the love my mother had for me today as I was then — and I'm even more grateful. The fine finish on that beautiful instrument has faded, but the faith she had in me remains. The dreams she encouraged are realities now.

Maybe you have a dream too. Whatever obstacles you face, do not settle for a second-hand piano when someone loves you enough to surprise you with a brand-new one. Whether your dream involves your job or your ministry or your marriage or your children or some other area of your life, God wants to do exceedingly abundantly more than you can ask. He is your father; He is your provider; He owns the cattle on a thousand hills; and He is the giver of every good and perfect gift.

Parents, when we are at our best, can model the heart of God for our children. I realize that, far too often, that is not the case. But we can choose to live with our children in such a way that we reflect His unconditional love, His tenderness, His grace, His mercy. What my mother did for me was only a shadow of God's heart. So much more than she wanted to give me the best, He longs to give good gifts to His children. So much more than she sacrificed, He sacrificed.

The sacrificial story begins with the star. God had a dream, too, you see. His dream has always been for us to do and be all He has created us to do and be — free from the bondage of sin and the baggage of painful pasts. And the dream could only be fulfilled at the Cross, when Jesus took the sins of the world upon Himself and died to redeem us and to set us free. The journey to the Cross began at the manger. Jesus is God's most extravagant gift. He was the day the star stood still, and He is today. God sent Him to earth to give us exceedingly abundant life. Some thirty years or so after His birth, Jesus Himself declares in John 10:10, "I have come that they may have life, and that they may have it more abundantly."

As you follow the Star this Christmas, see His exceeding abundance. Take the advice of Psalm 34:8 and "taste and see that the Lord is good!" Dust off those dreams and hold them up to the light of the One who loves you. Let them live again. I mean it: Whatever you do, don't let your dreams die. God has something in store that will do for you what that brand-new piano did for me.

So if you find yourself saying, "This will do. Really, this is fine," remember the piano. Don't ever settle for something less when God wants to give you the best.

4

You Have His Word on It

She was young and, no doubt . . . well . . . ordinary. Just a blushing adolescent, Mary probably did what other girls her age did, and daydreamed about the carpenter she planned to marry. Oh, the dreams she must have held in her heart as she thought about her life with Joseph — a wedding, a marriage, a home and, at some point, later, children.

I wonder if she heard him coming, or if he simply appeared. He was Gabriel the archangel, and he brought young Mary a life-changing, world-changing message from God:

Rejoice, highly favored one, the Lord is with you; blessed are you among women! . . . Do not be afraid, Mary, for you have found favor with God. And behold, you will conceive in your womb and bring forth a Son, and shall call His name Jesus. He will be great, and will be called the Son of the Highest; and the Lord God will give Him the throne of

His father David. And He will reign over the house of Jacob forever, and of His kingdom there will be no end.
LUKE 1:28; 30–33

Amid her awe, she had the good sense to bow respectfully before the angel, almost interrupting his good news with her question: "How can this be, since I do not know a man?" (Luke 1:34). I wonder if that was the Bible-time equivalent of, "You have got to be kidding. There is *no way.*" Can you imagine the fear that must have churned inside of her? Fear of what people would think, fear of what would happen to her body, fear of not being able to care for a child, and perhaps the most gripping fear of all — fear of whether her beloved Joseph would turn his back on her.

In the wake of the angel's startling announcement, Mary seemed unable to rest in what God had said. The Bible says that she was "troubled at his saying" (Luke 1:29). No doubt! Perhaps she struggled to believe because she could not see the source of such a blessing. Her human mind could not understand how it could happen to her, or to anybody, for that matter. Whoever heard of a pregnant virgin? Indeed, how *could* that be?

Truly, Mary found herself in an unbelievable situation. I mean, if ever something were impossible, this was it. I'm sure Mary meant no disrespect to her heavenly visitor, but I'm also sure she had to double-check — just to make sure he was aware that, biologically, there was no way such an event could occur. But, you know, that's what makes a miracle, a miracle.

Like Mary, I have known countless times when I could not believe the promise, though I tried with all of my heart. I remember a season of unemployment, knowing that God had promised to provide, to meet all of my needs but being unable to believe His word. I had to ask, "How can this be, since I have no job?" I can still remember when the electric company threatened to turn off the power at our house. I walked to the bus stop, counting out my change and with every step, hoping against hope that I could get there in time to persuade them to extend our service. All I could think was, *What will we do with two children and no lights in the house? How will we survive?*

I climbed aboard the bus, trying to smile at the other travelers, but my mind was far from pleasantries and cordial conversation. I was trying to muster my courage and fight my way through the deep foreboding sense of dread that kept rising up within me. I was feeling like I was too young to have so much to deal with. It wasn't fair, was it? I was at the end of my rope. As the bus chugged through the streets toward the electric company, more thoughts began to swirl: *If the plant had only stayed open another year, I wouldn't be in this shape.* . . . But, alas, I was, and there seemed little I could do.

I summoned my thoughts back from the depressing "if only's" and tried again to come up with a solution. But I had to be honest about the situation. I had no car; it had been repossessed when the unemployment ran out. No money; I'd lost my job months earlier and had no prospects for work in the near future. I was not only facing the loss of power at my house, I was already powerless as a person because there was absolutely nothing else I could do to try and help myself.

Bouncing along on the hard plastic seat of the bus, I sat smelling the fuel odors that wafted through the bus like toxic perfume and tried not to think what I was thinking. But I thought it anyway: *Where was God when I needed Him? Couldn't He see how hard I was trying? Didn't He know I had a wife and toddling twin boys to feed? Wasn't there some-*

thing He could do? Why wouldn't He come through for me?

After all, I was no stranger to hard work. I would have welcomed the opportunity to toil and sweat for an honest wage. But when the plant closed, hundreds of good, hard-working people descended upon the other employers in town and there simply were not enough jobs to go around. I was trying to be polite with God, but my faith was in the wringer and it was coming up dry!

I knew how Mary must have felt. There she was, pregnant through no fault of her own. She had an embarrassing situation imposed upon her by none other than God Himself. God isn't supposed to put us in a bind. He is supposed to get us out! But wait a minute. Who are we to say that Mary was really in a bad situation, despite the rumors and the scorn that would no doubt fly around Nazareth as soon as people found out? After all, the first words out of Gabriel's mouth when he greeted her were, "Rejoice, highly favored one, the Lord is with you: blessed are you among women!" As God's messenger, he spoke God's message — and God's message to Mary was, essentially, "You are one terrific young lady, and I have a very special purpose for your life. You are going to get to do something that will change the world, something no one else on earth will ever again have the privilege of doing. You will be honored above every other woman who will ever grace the face of the earth." And then, the promise that enables all of us to endure even the most difficult, most desperate circumstances: "The Lord is with you."

Isn't it true that the assurance of God's presence always makes us stronger? Isn't it true that, when we can say, "The Lord is with me," confidence begins to bubble up inside of us? When God calls us blessed, and when we know He is with us, even the seemingly bad situations take on purpose and become clothed in grace. When impossibilities line up in front of us like a firing squad, we simply have to get to the point that we can quiet our own souls enough to hear Him whisper, "I think you're terrific, and I'm right here with you." We have to open the Bible and read what He says. Things like, "I will not leave you nor forsake you" (Joshua 1:5), and "Be strong and of good courage; do not be afraid, nor be dismayed, for the Lord your God is with you wherever you go" (Joshua 1:9). When your marriage falls apart and so does the refrigerator, when the car won't start and the children won't behave, when all you can see is a disease or a divorce, those are the moments to remember His word. Those are good times for Romans 8:28, which promises that "we know that all things work together for good to those who love God, to those who are called according to His purpose."

You should know by now that God has a plan. And in His plan, there are all sorts of little pieces — situations, experiences, challenges, lessons — that somehow fit together to make one beautiful picture called your life. God is much more interested in seeing that the whole of your life all "works together for good" than He is in making sure that every circumstance is pleasant and that you lie down in a bed of roses every night.

If you have lived any time at all, you know that struggle is a part of life. You may have wondered how you will ever survive, and you may have asked, "How can this be?" But if you have walked with God any time at all, you also know that when He speaks, He acts. You know that what He says, He does. You know that when you have His word on something, you can count on Him to perform it.

I know these things too. As I have shared with you, I have had times in my life when I wanted to say, "I know what you mean, Mary. *How can this be?*" But I had grown up around God's word. I had read the rest of the story. I had seen another part of Gabriel's message that day and heard God speak as clearly to me as He did to Mary: "For with God, nothing will be impossible" (Luke 1:37).

Those words brought Mary to the turning point. Her pure heart was able to believe them. Fear fled; questions ceased; confidence came. Courage resounded in her response: "Behold the maidservant of the Lord! Let it be to me according to your word" (Luke 1:38).

I wonder what you are facing this Christmas. I wonder what is causing you to ask, "How can this be?" I want you to know that I understand the fears and the tears and the fact that you really do not know if you will make it. I want to say to you that you have God's word on your situation. I want to say to you what the angel said to Mary, "Do not be afraid. . . . For with God, nothing will be impossible."

5

Night-Lights

The kindergarten classroom was abuzz with activity and anticipation. It was December and we were going to do something special that day — we were making stars. Well, technically we were only drawing and decorating stars, because only the teachers were allowed to use the scissors to trim them out of the construction paper. We listened attentively to my mother, who happened to be our teacher, talk to us about drawing stars. All of us could count to five, she reminded us, and then she told us that our stars should have five points. She showed us how to slide our pencils across the paper — up and down, at all the appropriate angles — in order to make a picture-perfect, five-pointed star.

Now kindergarten is one of those things in life that never really changes. Among the cast of characters my mother instructed were some of the same types you may remember from your own experience. There was the rambunctious rascal of a little boy, who always required more than his share of the teacher's attention and constantly tried to corrupt the well-mannered boys by enticing them to join his mischief! There was also the beautiful maiden — the one with the frilly dresses and the long eyelashes and the soft, high-pitched voice. The rascal taunted her mercilessly, and she, of course, was terrified of him. There were children who showed intellectual or athletic giftings, and those whose early efforts revealed that school might always pose a challenge to them. There were some more privileged than others, and there were some whose stories would break your heart. There were the shy and the sociable, the serious and the silly. And there were the creative types — the ones who had rhythm, the ones who could sing, and ones who could draw. But on star day, *everybody* was an artist.

Even I felt like one of the Old Masters — a pintsized-Picasso maybe, or a mini-Monet — when I began to draw. I dedicated my young self zealously to my star-making until I had crafted the best star my little hand could possibly draw. One, two, three, four, five — yep, all the points were present. Finally satisfied, I presented my creation to my mother so that she could cut it out. As the teacher, showing favoritism would not have been very professional for her, but I could tell by the gleam in her eye that she thought I had made a very beautiful star indeed.

I returned to my seat and began to color my star. A smorgasbord of art supplies was available to us that day — crayons, markers, finger paints, tinfoil, and even glitter. By the time the entire class had finished drawing and coloring and gluing and glittering, we had a whole constellation drying on the windowsill. We all struggled to pay attention for the rest of the afternoon because we were so eager to see our finished work and take them home. I wasn't sure exactly what would become of my star once I got it home, but I knew that my mother would help me display it prominently, either on the refrigerator or, maybe, even on the Christmas tree. Yes, the Christmas tree — that was the perfect place for a star.

I don't know what ever happened to my childhood masterpiece. Even if it were buried in a box of memories somewhere, it would be old and yellowed and brittle by now. After all, for all of its glory, it was still only a paper star. It couldn't last forever.

Along my life's journey, I discovered a Star that does last forever, and His name is Jesus. I found a place as perfect for Him as the Christmas tree was for the star I made in my kindergarten. He belongs in my heart. His home is in the very kernel of my being. I look to Him for everything I need, and He shines brighter and brighter every day.

I'm not sure when I first saw the connection between the five-pointed stars we made so many years ago and the description of Jesus in Isaiah 9:6: "For unto us a Child is born, unto us a Son is given; and the government will be upon his shoulder. And His name will be called Wonderful, Counselor, Mighty God, Everlasting Father, Prince of Peace." These words do not paint a complete portrait of Jesus; there are not enough words in any language to adequately describe Him. But these five points — Wonderful, Counselor, Mighty God, Everlasting Father, Prince of Peace — do give us a glimpse of the King who was born over two thousand years ago. He has been all five, many times over, in my life.

You know, Jesus really is wonderful, and when something is wonderful, then it causes us to be full of wonder. That's what Jesus does. I can't help but wonder why He loves me so much that He died on the Cross to make sure that I wouldn't have to suffer over my own sins, but He did. I can't help but wonder why He always thinks the best about me, but He does. I can't help but wonder why He never gives up on me, but He doesn't. I can't help but wonder when I think about how thoroughly He heals broken hearts and how completely He restores wounded souls, but He does. I can't help but wonder when I try to consider how infinite His knowledge is and how perfect His plans are for every single person on the face of the earth, but that's the truth. He is so wonderful, so pure, so awesome in His love for us. There is nothing but goodness in Jesus, and everything He does is born out of a love that is larger than anything the human mind can comprehend. So what do we do when we encounter something we cannot comprehend? Well, we just fall into the wonder of it.

Jesus is also the Counselor. There was a time when any kind of counseling was only spoken of in whispers, and people who received therapy were looked down upon by others. Oh, how things change! In our modern society, therapy is in vogue. People discuss their "issues" and their counseling sessions as casually as they do the weather, and if you don't want to visit a therapist yourself, you can find one on television and get help while sitting on your sofa instead of the doctor's proverbial couch! But I must tell you that counselors are only human —

even the well-known, highly paid celebrity therapists on TV. None of them knows you as intimately as Jesus; none of them loves you as purely; none of them can cut to the heart of your issues and diagnose you with such accuracy and precision. None of them can heal you; only Jesus.

I often make decisions that will impact large numbers of people, and when I do, I pay a visit to the Counselor. I seek His wisdom and His perspective. And He always leads me down the right path. That is not to say that I do everything perfectly. Sometimes I stumble as I follow, but He always leads well.

I remember one time — a grueling season for our family — when I needed Him desperately as my Counselor. My mother-in-law had passed away and her departure impacted my wife deeply. I did not know how to comfort the woman I love. I could not sing enough songs to make her smile or give her enough flowers to fill the gap in her heart. I could not take her on a vacation, because her grief followed her wherever she went. I tried everything, but nothing worked. Then I asked the Counselor, and He taught me — gradually, steadily, and thoroughly — how to let Him love her back to life.

As tender as He is when He functions as our Counselor, Jesus is that powerful when He shows up as the Mighty God. There is absolutely nothing He cannot do. He is the one who moves mountains with His fingertip and calms the raging waves with one holy whisper. There is no obstacle He cannot obliterate; no deterrent He cannot demolish. He causes the dead to live again; He restores the soul; He heals the sick; and He makes the lame leap for joy. May I tell you a secret? I am not speaking theoretically here; I have personally encountered Him in every way I have described to you. My mountains have been figurative and my storms often spiritual; nevertheless, His power has been exactly what I needed when I needed it, and I can tell you with authority that He is the Mighty God.

I was only sixteen years old when my natural father slipped into eternity. I stood beside his grave wrestling with the crushing reality that my daddy was gone. Oh, we knew it was coming, but that didn't make the loss any less profound. He fought kidney disease for years, and it slowly but surely ravaged his tall, muscular body until he could fight it no more. I did everything I could to help him — feeding him, washing him, talking to him. All I wanted, every day, was to hold onto him just a little longer. I was no different from anybody else; I needed a father. And after he passed, I had nowhere to turn but toward heaven.

What I discovered was a new dimension of the God I knew as Lord and Savior. I found Him as my Father — the One who loves me so much I can hardly believe it; the One who teaches me how to live and corrects me gently; the One who arranges the opportunities I need — and makes sure I am ready for them; the One whose patience never runs dry; the One who cheers me on; the One who gives me access to all of His endless resources; the One who still welcomes me to climb onto His lap when I need to, even though I am grown; the One who says, "Well done" (that's Bible language for "Atta boy!") at the end of the day.

The fifth of the five points is that Jesus is the Prince of Peace. I don't know why Isaiah put that last, but I do know that when everything else is said and done, we need to have a sense of peace. When the Prince of Peace appears on the scene, the demons of fear and anxiety and depression have to flee. When He comes into a situation, He brings order to confusion and infuses even the tensest moment with, "Everything's going to be all right."

Jesus has been my Peace-Giver in some humdinger storms of life. But He has not only brought peace to those intense times, He has also wrapped the shawl of His unshakable serenity around the busyness and the stress of everyday living. He brings such calmness to the large ministry that takes place at a fast pace around our church. He makes me able to breathe when I am trying to do too many things in not enough time. And He doesn't play favorites; the kind of peace He brings to my life is the kind of peace He wants to bring to yours.

You know what? My mom is in heaven, and I am not a child anymore. I have good days and bad. But the answer to a question I asked Mom that star-making day in kindergarten always helps me cope with life.

"Momma, why did God make stars?" I asked.

Now you need to know, my mother was never one to be left speechless. She looked at me and smiled. A hush of wonder fell over the whole classroom as she calmly and quickly replied, "Because, He knew it would get dark sometimes, and when it did you would need a night-light."

I am grown now, and I still ask a lot of questions. But I never ask God why He made stars. There have been too many times I needed a night-light. Now I don't think real stars have only five points, but these five points have often helped me see the light when I was walking in a dark, dark night.

I hope you'll take a moment this Christmas to gaze upon Jesus and let yourself be filled with wonder. I hope you'll seek the advice of the Counselor and experience the power of the Mighty God. I hope you'll know Him intimately as your Everlasting Father and that His reign of Peace will rest upon you and your household this holiday season. If it gets dark at any time throughout the coming year, remember that God always turns on the night-light for His children!

6

Angels Watching Over Me, My Lord

I heard the laughter like cymbals crashing boisterously beneath the bedroom window. The children were outside — never mind how cold it was — laughing and playing and having fun. Snowballs were being hurled with the kind of force that would have made you think they hated each other. A snowball slammed into a window and everything went silent. To the boys' unspeakable relief, the window didn't break, but it was too close.

"Stop it!" I shouted. "Stop it before I have to come out there!"

Their winter wonderland was not as much fun anymore, and their snow party seemed to be over. My two boys had dropped their heads and were peeking out from behind their toboggans toward me, in search of the slightest sign of mercy. There was none.

Jermaine broke their joint sadness with an announcement: "I know what to do. We will get the angel to talk to Daddy."

"What angel?" Jamar asked.

"This one!" Jermaine shouted with glee. Without another word, he dropped down into a pile of snow and started flailing his arms. He was in the early stages of making his angels. Still frowning, I walked outside to watch until he had completed his snowy masterpiece.

I think now about how resourceful my little boy was that day so many years ago, and about how quickly he found a solution to his problem. I remember the delight on his face and the carefree sound in his voice once he created that mighty fine snow angel. I will admit that I was most unhappy about the snowball and the window, but my heart could not help but soften when I saw the angel!

Isn't it funny how children can summon angels from snowstorms? They don't even seem to notice that the temperature is freezing and their noses are running and their lips are almost blue. As I walked back into the house that day, I thought, *It isn't really cold if you can make angels come out of your snowstorms.*

You may have faced some snowstorms of your own. Perhaps you have made some mistakes or even truly failed at something. Maybe you have hurt someone you love or been hurt by them. You might have been scolded or criticized or falsely accused. You may have too much month and not enough money, or a heavy heart that seems like it will never heal. Maybe the ones you love haven't been around for a while — or are causing so much pain that you sometimes wish they weren't around! You might have a pile of problems that seems like Mt. Everest, and you don't think you can ever get on top of it. These are life's storms, and they blow into all of our lives in some form or another. So I would like to make a suggestion next time the cold winds invade your life and the snowdrifts arise: Perhaps you should do like the children and make angels show up in spite of your storm.

There is nothing quite as exhilarating to a child as a snow day. Children keep watch at the windowsill when snow is in the forecast. With their noses pressed against the panes, they try to keep their bubbling excitement from exploding as they squint and strain just hoping to catch a glimpse of the flakes falling from the sky. At the first sign of the white stuff, the children are bundled up and out the door, rushing headlong into the flurry with the perfect understanding that snow days are a gift to be treasured and maximized and enjoyed until their little legs can't waddle anymore through the soft, white blanket that covers the ground, and until they've made themselves sick on snow ice cream!

But something happens to us as we grow up. We begin to get nervous when those little snowflakes appear on the weather map while we're watching the evening news. Perhaps adulthood, maturity, and responsibility suck the joy out of a snow day. Whatever the reason, something happens as we get older, and it causes snow to be a source of dread instead of delight.

Yes, a grown person sees a snowstorm and wonders how he will get to work. *Oh great,* he thinks. *I'll have to get up early and scrape the stuff off my windshield and then leave early to make it to the office on time. And nobody in this town knows how to drive in the snow anyway. It'll probably take me four hours to get home tonight.* We adults worry about the inconveniences and the dangers of having to be out and about during a blizzard. We certainly hope the city is on top of the matter and that the salt trucks have made their rounds in short order. We want to know if the sidewalks are slippery because we don't have time for an injury in our busy lives.

To those of us with more than a few birthdays under our belts, snowstorms mean challenges and accidents and all sorts of potential trouble. But to the children, to boys like mine, snowstorms mean a chance to make angels appear. We walk gingerly across snow-covered driveways and parking lots, struggling to keep our balance. Children jump into the snow expecting to fall (that's the whole point). We try to stand up and they laughingly lie down! Giggling and gleeful, they fall down and wave their arms and legs and make angels appear.

I remember doing this myself as a young boy, and oh, it was so much fun! I plopped down in every snow pile I could find and flailed wildly until the indentation my arms made in the snow looked just like angels' wings. Isn't it beginning to seem silly to you that, now that we are grown, we think more about the traffic than we do the chance to make angels? Maybe, just maybe, if we took a lesson from the young ones and learned how to make angels, life would not be so threatening.

Over and over and over again, the Bible teaches us not to worry; and yet, so many times we do. Jesus Himself said things like: "Therefore I say to you, do not worry about your life, what you will eat or what you will drink; nor about your body, what you will put on. . . . Look at the birds of the air, for they neither sow nor reap nor gather into barns; yet your heavenly Father feeds them. Are you not of much more value than they?" (Matthew 6:25–26), and "Consider the lilies of the field, how they grow; they neither toil nor spin; and yet I say to you that even Solomon in all his glory was not arrayed like one of these" (Matthew 6:28–29). In the Old Testament, that wise King Solomon said that "anxiety in the heart of man causes depression" (Proverbs 12:25), and in the New Testament, the apostle Paul encourages us to "be anxious for nothing" (Philippians 4:6).

Nevertheless, when dark clouds begin to gather, those biblical instructions (which are intended to help us) seem to be forgotten and our first thought tends to be, *Oh God, a storm is coming!* We end up in panic, with anxious thoughts swirling inside of us more than the winds are swirling outside! We worry about what will happen and who will be hurt. Not so for the children. No, the children, who think they are invulnerable and immune to tragedy, run headfirst into the storm, laughing and playing. Meanwhile, for us, the tension mounts.

I hope we will all turn back to the Bible

this Christmas and take Jesus' good advice and refuse to worry in the midst of our storms. While He was on earth, He continually taught people how to overcome troubles in their lives, and He calmed a few storms of His own. Hundreds of years before He ever showed up in the stable as a baby, God told people through the prophet Isaiah what His name would be and what He would be able to do in the lives of men and women just like you: "And His name will be called Wonderful, Counselor, Mighty God, Everlasting Father, Prince of Peace" (Isaiah 9:6).

Isn't it encouraging to realize that the Star we follow is the Prince of Peace? Isn't it good to know He is in control and we really don't need to worry about anything at all? I want the Prince of Peace to reign in your heart. I want those anxieties and worries to fall off of you like dead limbs off of a tree. I want there to be a twinge of excitement in your heart when you see snowflakes on the weather forecast. As a grown-up, I hope you will savor the peace of a snow-covered hill, for few things blanket the earth with peace like a snowfall does. But as a child — because I know there's one in you somewhere — I hope that when you peer out your window this winter and see the snowflakes, you will throw on your coat and grab your mittens and fall into a pile of white, flailing your arms with all your might and make an angel out of your storm.

7

Bringing in the Sheaves

I could hardly believe my eyes when I saw it. It was the most beautiful, soft, solid white coat I had ever seen — and it seemed tailor-made for my wife. I was in New York City and was able to negotiate a great price on the coat, so I took it home — all excited — and hid it until I could present it to my wife on Christmas morning. I could hardly wait to see how it looked on her.

Finally, the moment arrived. As anticipated, she oohed and aahed over the coat and then handed it to me to hold for her as she put it on. I felt like her knight in shining armor and was as thrilled as she was about the coat. She modeled it for us — the four children and me — beside the Christmas tree in the living room of our ranch-style home in West Virginia. The children thought the coat was wonderful, but all four of their faces assumed puzzled looks as they inspected her wrapped in my gift.

"It's a nice coat, Mom," they observed, "but it doesn't fit you too good."

They were right. Her gorgeous coat was gaping open in the front. It wouldn't close because we had just recently found out that she was expecting!

"Yes, I know," she responded.

My wife has always been the kind of woman who seemed to gain weight the night she got pregnant, but the children hadn't really noticed and were totally shocked when she responded, "Yes, I know," and we proceeded to let them know that a new sibling was on the way.

What a Christmas morning that was! All of us so excited, rejoicing together over the new baby. The children soon began doting on their mother and scolding me as though the entire situation were my fault. It wasn't — we just stayed in Hawaii on vacation a little bit too long! To this day, they tease us and laugh about Mom's white coat!

I still smile when I think about that moment — tree lights blinking, my wife beaming (in the coat that didn't fit), the children gathered around her waiting their turn to touch her belly, and all of us sensing the wonder of it all. It was a marvelous Christmas. What better announcement for a family to make and celebrate on Christmas morning than the upcoming birth of a child? We couldn't see him; we couldn't feel him; we didn't even know if he might be a she. But Dexter was coming, and to me he was a gift worth waiting for.

Now, it took him until August to get here, but it was Christmas morning that we told the story. During the following months, all we could see was my wife's expanding midsection, but that was enough to let us know that he was still there, that he was growing, and that he was getting ready for the day we would finally see him.

Notice that he was conceived in December but born in August. My wife and I had to carry into a new year a seed that was planted in the previous year. We could announce Dexter's impending arrival, but we could do absolutely nothing to force it into reality. Life is like that, you know, and God's purposes for our lives are the same way. We cannot make them happen. We must carry them; we must allow them to develop; we must labor and we must deliver them at the right time.

All of this makes me think of the old hymn entitled "Bringing in the Sheaves." Do you know this joyful tune? "Bringing in the sheaves, bringing in the sheaves. We shall come rejoicing bringing in the sheaves!" Sheaves were nothing more than bundles of wheat that had been gathered in the fields, so the song speaks of harvest time. You know that wheat does not get planted and harvested in the same season. No, there is all the time that the little seed is invisible under the soil, then it breaks through and begins to grow until it is finally mature enough to be harvested so that it can be useful. One little seed is not nearly as useful as a full stalk of wheat. That seed has the potential to be of great benefit, but not until it is nourished by the soil and water and bathed in the sunlight. The seed undergoes total transformation as it moves from one season to the next and then to the fall harvest. It is like Dexter on that Christmas morning. He was a gift to us, but we would have to wait nine months before we could unwrap him!

Maybe you are carrying a dream that cannot be unwrapped right now. Maybe you are pregnant with unrealized potential, gifting, and purpose that must be processed before they can be enjoyed. Remember that you don't have to have the fulfillment to announce the promise. The angel announced to Mary that she would bring forth — and she did. My wife carried Dexter in the safety of her womb for nine long months, but in due time, she brought forth. Like Mary and like my wife, you, too, will bring forth if you nurture your potential. Whatever you do, don't give up!

A woman knows she is pregnant before a medical test ever gives her confirmation. Destiny is the same way — you just know that certain dreams are going to become reality in your life; you just know that certain things will come to pass. No one can convince you otherwise. You may not know when, you may not know how, but in the bottom of your heart — *you know*.

Now there may be weeks or months or years between the time you sense destiny stirring within you and the time you see it happen in your life. A gestation period is not unusual at all; it is a part of the life cycle of every living thing. The only difference is that you are not likely to know exactly how long you will have to wait. All I can promise you is that when God plants a seed in your heart, He goes to work preparing you for its full bloom, and He causes it to spring forth at precisely the right moment. He waters you; He strengthens you; He sends your roots deep. In the process, you will find that you don't always understand His ways, and you may become frustrated with the wait. Do not let your destiny die, because I assure you, you do not want a premature baby. You want a full-term, dream-come-true to show the world.

I want to ask you a few questions. The fact that I probably will not ever hear your answers is beside the point. I am asking you because *you* need to hear the answers. What are you carrying? What is inside of you? Are you paying attention to the way it's growing and moving around in you? Are you preparing yourself for its fulfillment?

I want to encourage you to take care of yourself and to be vigilant over the dream inside of you. Just as a wise pregnant woman disciplines herself not to eat certain foods or engage in certain activities, you will also want to nourish your dream with healthy things and refrain from attitudes and relationships that could harm the seed within you. Just as an expectant mother tries to make sure she gets enough rest, make sure that the burdens of life do not wear you out and cause you to become cranky and discouraged. Just as a pregnant woman often feels the liberty to pamper herself and treat herself well because of her condition, I hope you will consider yourself worth a reasonable splurge and will indulge. You may not be a pregnant woman — you may be a middle-aged man — but you are carrying something precious too!

Are you at the point where you should be

painting the nursery and buying a car seat? Or have you so recently conceived that it really isn't time for that yet? Maybe you are close to delivery or maybe you are still trying to get over the shock that there is actually brand-new life in you. Regardless, I know it's there. I want you to tune in and discover where you are on your destiny's journey. That way, you can better prepare.

In the midst of the shopping and the wrapping and the arranging of presents under your tree this Christmas, may you not forget the gifts you cannot yet hold in your hands. May you remember the invisible treasures that can only be gazed upon in the privacy of your own soul. Come on, dust off those dreams. In fact, blow on them and tell them to live again! 'Tis the season! Come rejoicing, my sister! Come rejoicing, my brother! And get ready to bring in your sheaves!

8

Burning Down the Old School

The blending together of my wife and me consists of so much more than two lovers finding their way through the wind-tossed world into each other's arms, where they will spend a lifetime recovering from the gusty gales that drew them together in the first place. It is more than two Christians whose destinies, from the foundations of the world, were meant to be intertwined for divine Kingdom-building. It is even more than God's bilateral partnership designed to birth our children into the world and model for them the commitment and love we have for each other. It is also the combining of traditions and ideas.

You see, my family and my wife's family are totally different and, when we married, her ideas of a great Christmas were totally different from mine. Some of the traditions we brought into our union are really carryovers from each of our childhoods. She and I quickly realized that our respective customs worked well together. They mixed like a carefully blended cup of coffee, and we were able to enjoy the fresh aroma of our concocted experiences — until our children were old enough to verbalize their preferences!

For my wife, Christmas is a time for lights and decorations. Opulent ornamentation graces our home. Weeks are spent decking the halls and trimming the tree, and the magic and beauty of this joyous season is reflected in the festive and comfortable atmosphere my wife creates for our family and our guests who visit for the holiday.

For me, however, Christmas is marked by hard work in the kitchen and extra-special meals that are anticipated all year long. It is characterized by feasting and eggnog and roaring fires and stockings that are hung by the chimney with care! But one day I noticed that our children were not impressed with those traditional trappings of Christmas, which had meant so much to us. I felt myself getting frustrated by their lack of enthusiasm, and by the time I had seen them snub the holiday feast and run to McDonald's for the second day in a row — well, then I was thoroughly frustrated. All I could think about was my own childhood, when the excitement built up and then lasted for days over eating the fine cooking and scrumptious cakes and pies. I remembered how totally satisfied and happy we were to lie on the floor playing with new toys, or to provide a fashion show for the family while modeling new clothes. This was not the case for our children. Initially they seemed excited about the meals and the opportunity to sit around the Christmas tree enjoying gifts, but boredom snuck up on them quickly and they decided to stick a Walkman in their ears and head for the movie theater and a hot dog. Man, was I insulted!

But, do you know something? I had to rethink my position. I had to remember how different my upbringing was from theirs. I was raised on "Mayberry R.F.D." and "The Brady Bunch." I grew up when people were still afraid of microwave ovens because we thought they might give us cancer. My childhood was filled with foods my children never heard of, foods like tomato sandwiches, cheese sandwiches, sugar sandwiches, and all sorts of delicacies that might cause my children to turn up their noses.

Except for the twins, when they were young, our children had grown up with steak dinners, restaurants, church suppers, and people bringing over home-cooked breads and the like. I began to understand

95

why Christmas dinner was clearly not the highlight to them that it was to me. After all, they had school clothes, name-brand jeans, and things that I would have never dared to ask for. The children didn't appreciate our old traditions because they were from the new school and we were from the old one — which somebody burned down in order to build the new one!

My wife and I decided to talk to our children about the generation gap we found ourselves in as we tried to celebrate Christmas. When we asked them what was important to them, they said the oddest thing. Their unanimity was astounding! They all agreed, immediately, and said to us, "What we want most for Christmas is to go where no phones ring, no people come over, no meetings are scheduled, and we have your total, undivided attention for a week." I was shocked! No new Nintendo! No latest gadgets. For Christmas, all they were asking for was *us*. Isn't that amazing?

My children's simple request reminded me of how we are with God. Living in a fast-paced, technology-driven, get-it-done, status-symbol world, we often find ourselves dedicated to acquiring the things that make us look like we want to look and feel like we want to feel. When we fail to acquire them in our own strength, we ask God for them. So many times, we simply are not quiet enough to realize that a new dress cannot cover up a broken heart or that a new car cannot take us to a place of peace. I believe that what we are really thirsting for is time alone with Him. What we are really yearning for is that private moment when we can be touched by His love and healed by His merciful grace. What we are longing for is an encounter with Him — an encounter that restores our hope, relieves the pressure of our stress-filled lives, and revives our weary day-to-day existence.

I would like to ask you a question: What would you say if God were to ask you, "What is it that you really want?" I want you to drill down to the depth of your soul — past the material goods, past the things you could do for yourself, past even anything that money can buy. What is it that your innermost being really cries out for? Has the busyness of your life silenced the desires of your heart? It's time for them to begin to breathe again; it's time for them to make their presence known inside of you again. It's time to take a step back from contemporary culture and media-influenced society and think about what really matters to *you*. I ask you, what is it that only God can do in your life?

As I pondered this scenario of God stopping us in our tracks and saying, "What is it that you really want?" I realized why relationships often fail. Many times we are so busy giving people what we thought they wanted that we do not stop to really learn what they want. This time of year, we often give people the things that represent our love, rather than showering them with the love itself. Almost always, what means the most is not the gift with the beautiful bow but the beautiful person who gives it. As nice as things can be, they are not nearly as nice as the people who hand them to us out of love. Your grandmother may ooh and aah over that new robe and even the slippers to match, but what she would really treasure is an afternoon with you. I'll bet you that everybody on your Christmas list wants to be loved, valued, appreciated, and to know that you are interested in them, more than they want something else to hang in the closet or display in the living room. I'll bet the same is true for you.

Just as it thrilled me beyond words to hear my children say, "We just want to be with you," those same words thrill God. He loves to hear you say, "I just want to be with you." I want to tell you this Christmas that God is listening to you. His ear is turned in your direction, and He is eager to hear you express your desires. Go ahead, tell Him what you want — and rejoice in the fact that you do not have to be like anyone else. You can ask Him for that which would add meaning to your life now — and that may not be the same thing that might have brought meaning to your life years ago. You may need to update your traditional prayer and allow God to do a new thing in you.

Believe me, God is in the business of doing new things. I have seen Him remake so many lives and do such wonders in people that they really are able to shake off the past and become new. In the prophecy of Isaiah, God says, "Behold, the former things have come to pass, and new things I declare. . . ." (Isaiah 42:9), and "Do not remember the former things, nor consider the things of old. Behold, I will do a new thing" (Isaiah 43:18–19). My friend, He will do a new thing for you if you'll ask Him.

In order to enjoy the new thing, you will have to let go of the old. I had to let go of the frustration I felt when my offspring did not burst into "Joy to the World" at the sight of Christmas dinner. But only in releasing that could I embrace the joy of giving them the whole week of undivided attention they wanted from their mother and me. In fact, one of the ways I follow the Star not only at Christmas but all year long is to make sure that I never grip the past too tightly. I always allow enough space between my fingers for the old things to slip away so that I can grasp and hold the fresh, new work of God in my life.

With the new year just around the corner, you may already be thinking in terms of goals and dreams and things you want to accomplish. Sometimes we get so entrenched in the patterns of our lives that we end up in a full-blown rut before we know it, so now is a good time to open yourself up to a fresh, new work of God in your life too. Maybe it's also time to reevaluate your priorities and to take a few moments to look deeply into your own heart, be honest about what you really long for, and do not be afraid to ask for a new thing.

9

Be Careful What You Wish For

The wide-eyed little girl can hardly wait to go to the mall and see Santa Claus. She puts on her frilly Christmas dress and her Sunday shoes, brimming with excitement about seeing the man in the red, furry suit. She does her best to be patient as she waits in line behind the other children — some who are no doubt as excited as she is, some who look completely unimpressed, and others who appear downright frightened.

Then it hits her: She is supposed to tell him what she wants for Christmas. After all, he is the one who will slide down her chimney on Christmas Eve and deliver the goods. She needs to decide what to ask him to leave for her — and quickly. The pressure mounts with every step she takes toward the painted wooden platform, where he receives his guests and takes their requests (miraculously, without ever writing anything down!).

She runs out of time. A woman motions her to come forward. Casting a glance at her mother nearby, all she hears is, "Go on. Go on. Go tell him what you want for Christmas." The problem is that she really doesn't know. So, not wanting to seem unprepared for her annual moment with Santa Claus, she makes up something. She says the first thing she can think of, even though she really doesn't want that at all. When Santa responds with a kind smile and an indication that he will do as she has asked, she isn't excited anymore. She slides off of his large lap and returns to her mother, not looking forward to Christmas at all because, well, now she's going to get a silly old doll she doesn't even want.

Does that scenario ring any bells for you? Have you ever approached the throne of grace and asked God for something simply because someone else has it? Have you ever wanted a car or a boat or an item of clothing because your friend had one? Maybe you've got the material goods under control, but you wish you had the kind of confidence she exhibits or the ability to command respect the way he does. Perhaps you even wish God had called and equipped you for the ministry for which He has called and equipped your best friend. Even though you know in your gut that He hasn't, you ask Him anyway.

I must confess, I did something similar myself one time. I didn't really ask God for it — not in terms of hard-core prayer and seeking His will — but I did have the sense that He wanted to do a new thing in our family and perhaps I overstepped my bounds as I thought I knew precisely what our blessing should be.

I had heard about families who took fabulous holiday vacations, so, realizing that the children were serious about wanting nothing more for Christmas than uninterrupted time with their parents, I decided to plan an unforgettable holiday getaway. Some went skiing, others went shopping in New York City, but what set off a spark in me was the opportunity to enjoy a warm, surfside holiday with balmy breezes and sunshine and a little adventure on the water. Instead of visions of sugarplums, my mind's eye saw scenes of the seven of us stretched out on deck chairs, sailing through the Pacific, resting, at peace with ourselves and one another.

We were all going to Hawaii. Armed with about a billion frequent-flier points, two credit cards, and some suntan lotion (yes, black people do need suntan lotion!), we were off to the beautiful islands in the sea. We were doing a new thing, tossing aside the hand-me-down customs of our past and establishing a new and unique family tradition. None of us had ever taken our family vacation at Christmastime or spent the holidays at the beach. Going to Hawaii was fresh — and that was just exactly what we all needed. I braced myself for the inevitable complaining that was sure to be unleashed once the children recognized the lack of gifts and such and remained unconvinced that they would be happy with the absence of snow and sleds, eggnog and dressing with giblet gravy. (Do you know what? They had a ball and never brought it up.)

The highlight of my plan was to spend Christmas Day on the high seas. I had rented a small boat and was going to give Serita and the children the time of their lives. What a glorious way to spend Christmas! We awakened that morning bursting with excitement over our new adventure and, as I said, no one ever uttered a word about the fact that we had no presents. Soon, we were ready to go. We were, after all, in Hawaii, and I was starting to really enjoy this new world of new traditions. With a cooler full of food, a boom box for music, some games in case we were bored, aspirin, first aid kits, etc., we headed down to the ocean, where a boat was waiting on the dock. This was going to be great. The children were all singing and laughing, and my wife and I were sitting on top of the world. It was Christmas and we had on shorts. We were radical. We were breaking all the rules, letting our hair down, hanging out and living dangerously! It was great.

We arrived at the boat and met the captain and his wife. He was all smiles. Once on board, he gave us a quick tour of the little boat and we were ready to go. By the way, I chose not to think about a scene I had observed as we climbed onto the boat. My wife and the girls seemed a little uncomfortable with the fact that the boat was not still as they moved onto it from the dock. It was wobbling, as boats do, but after a moment of balancing on the edge of the dock, all three of them had leapt onto the vessel with shouts of glee. *Just a little preboating nervousness,* I thought, *but all is well now and here we go.*

Within a few minutes, I could hear the engines turning, smell the ocean breeze, and feel the morning air brushing against my face. The seagulls were welcoming us, and we were literally singing Christmas carols as we floated away from the dock. "Hark! The herald angels sing," we chimed, "Glory to the newborn King! Peace on earth, and mercy mild, God and sinners reconciled!" The island in the distance was growing smaller as we motored away, and by the time the engines were at full throttle, there were only a few specks of land in sight. It was nothing but us and the ocean. While my wife and the other children were all inside the boat, below deck, my youngest son, Dexter, and I were playing Gilligan and Skipper above.

"Shiver me timbers!" I shouted.

"Land, ho!" he yelled.

Neither one of us had a clue what we were talking about, but boy, was it fun! This was going to be a terrific day. Not only did I get to act like Skipper, I was taking a class on how to catch the *big* fish. When we finished playing, I was going to get serious for a little while, determined to return to shore with at least a seven-foot mackerel!

Bless my soul, about twenty minutes into the trip, I noticed that my wife and the children had stopped singing. The boat was rocking gently, the wind still blowing lightly. It was a beautiful Christmas, but I didn't hear much noise down there. Seems there was just a little, tiny problem. One of the children was feeling a little queasy, but we were prepared for that. We whipped out the motion-sickness pills, prayed the prayer of faith, and kept on going. After all, faith without works is dead, right? *Thank goodness that's all it was,* I thought. *She'll be fine once that medicine takes effect.*

Back on deck, Dexter and I continued our adventure. Dexter was having such a great time he could hardly stop playing long enough to go downstairs to get us something to eat. But he finally did, and he returned with a strange look on his face and a message I didn't want to hear: "Daddy, something is wrong down there." When I went downstairs to evaluate the situation for myself, every one of our family members was turning the deepest shade of green you have ever seen. My wife was hanging on to the side of the boat, and she was blue-green. Others were sort of dark yellow-green. Everyone was nauseated except Dexter and me.

Then I really started praying. One, I wanted my family to be well; and two, I had spent a chunk on this boat and I was going to get the big fish. We were not turning around and spending Christmas on land!

"Bless them, Lord," I said, "and keep on sailing, Captain!"

My prayer/pep talk was interrupted by the grinding of a stomach shifting into reverse. I looked around and saw eyes starting to get glassy. "Find a focal point!" I instructed. "Focus on that island in the distance." (It wasn't working.) "Focus now, this is going to pass."

I will spare you the gory details of the remainder of our adventure at sea, but suffice it to say that our day turned into the Christmas from hell. They were all sick — all but Dexter and me. I could hardly bear to see Dexter so disappointed when I finally gave in and told the captain to take us back to shore, but I really had no choice. By the time we were back on land, the money was lost, and I never even got my chance to hook that mackerel. But at least my family members were turning back to their normal colors.

I learned the difference that day between a good idea and a God-idea. Sometimes we really mean well, but every idea isn't a good idea and every good idea isn't necessarily a God-idea. You see, my friend, one man's dream is another man's nightmare. Be careful what you ask for and refuse to envy other people's lives.

I had always wanted to see what it was like out there on the sea. I may still go again. But if I do, I am going alone. This harpoon stuff was not for everybody; it sure wasn't for us. We had a wonderful holiday once we recovered. We really did, but we certainly learned from our experience. I may go back to Hawaii, but this seafaring Skipper doesn't want to end up playing Florence Nightingale to a bunch of sick shipmates.

I want this story to encourage you to know yourself; be happy with yourself; discover what God has for *you*. Allow Him to do things that are tailored to who you are and what He has for your life. Seek the new things that He wants to give and not the ones you think you'd enjoy. And whatever you do, be careful what you ask for — you just might get it!

10

Little Things

It was a normal "day at the ranch" for me —
both the cell phones were ringing, business
booming, stock fluctuating, emails backed
up, problems to be solved, and contracts to
be reviewed. I had been busy not only with
my pastoral duties; I was also vacillating between church work and the various entrepre-
neurial pursuits I am involved in. I was trying
to focus on our growing record label and
looking over a possible script for a gospel play
that we were considering launching across
the country. Busy with the responsibilities al-
located to me, it was easy to get distracted
and forget about the package I received in the
mail. Even though it was from one of my relatives, I set it on the table and decided to look
at it later. I was too busy, I thought, to even
open the box, so I don't know how long it sat
there on the table before I finally went to see
what was inside.

I took the heavy, tightly sealed box in my
hands, with my mind fried (as it often is
when I have overloaded the little database I

call a brain). I stared at the return address distractedly, almost not recognizing my aunt's return address or her unmistakable handwriting. It hadn't changed. It was still the same, but when you have too much on your plate, you can get kind of dazed after a while.

My aunt had wrapped it like it might be breakable — the way older people do when they send you something in the mail. It was clad with layers of brown paper and at least a roll of tape in every conceivable direction. Therefore, it took awhile to open it! There was no wrapping paper on it, but it was obviously a Christmas gift from her to me. We were in the midst of that time of year when we let people we know that we remember them.

As the pastor of a thriving church, I was not short on gifts for Christmas. Because so many people know me only in a ministry context, I generally end up with quite a few pictures of Jesus or with pictures, murals, and plates with the Last Supper in all shapes and sizes. I have them with black disciples and white disciples. I have every possible picture of Jesus — sitting in the field, knocking at the door, coming out of the tomb, doing everything but getting a shave in the barbershop!

I certainly don't mean to make light of these gifts because they come from the heart of loving people who want to include me on their Christmas "to-do" list. I have to admit that it can be difficult to shop for me; everybody says so. It is difficult for people who only know me as a pastor to figure out what I need, because they really don't interact with me outside of a church setting. It is even a challenge for my children to determine what to give me for Christmas, partially because they are on a budget and partially because it has been alleged that I am picky, though I plead innocent of all such charges. Christmas shopping for me is even difficult for my wife because, in the twenty-something years we have been married, we have given each other about everything you could think of — including a few gray hairs! (Shhhh! Don't tell her I said that.) Seriously, it is hard to buy for certain people, and some say that I have everything. They don't seem to realize that no one has everything. People have voids no matter who they are; you just have to look for them.

As far as creative shopping was concerned, I wasn't getting high marks in that department either. I was so busy that I had failed to get my own shopping done, and I thought I might have to resort to the old faithful gifts — fruit baskets, gift certificates, and other items designed for people who are too busy to shop. There are on-line services that provide a chance for you to log on to the computer, view pictures of the various gifts available, choose one with a click of your mouse, pay by credit card, and have the beautifully wrapped gift appear at the door of the one for whom you purchased it. I was tempted to take advantage of the time-saving advantages of technology. After all, time was of the essence and there were book deadlines, funerals, weddings, board meetings, and on and on and on. *Who has time to shop?* I thought. *Who has time to do anything anymore?*

Those were the thoughts rumbling around in my overworked head as I rambled through the drawers for scissors. *It must be a bomb,* I mused, noting the way it was wrapped. When I finally did get it open, a layer of newspaper hid the contents from view. I wrestled through the paper to see what had been sent to me and there inside lay a hidden treasure. It was a box filled to the brim with pecans. Now you have to understand that these were not store-bought, prepackaged pecans that come already shelled and ready to eat. These are the pecans that come the way God made them

— wrapped in their shells, fresh as can be. I knew, judging from the relative who sent them, that they had come from the yard in front of her house. She had taken time to gather them and box them up and send them through the mail to make sure I had them. My auntie knew that I liked pecans, and she decided to make sure that I had what I wanted.

This was not a woman who based her gift-giving decision on her experience with me behind a pulpit or on a television screen. No, it was based on the child I was when I was around her more often than I am now. She still saw me as that barefoot little boy from up north who came down to see her in the summer. I was a lanky-legged, toothless wonder, smiling through my gums and mischievous as you please! (I could easily be blackmailed now with one of those childhood pictures that only a mother would keep!) Boy, I had come a long way from those simple days of frolic and carefree living. No question about it; the little boy is all grown up now.

My aunt knew I had liked fresh pecans as a child, and in her mind I would always be that boy running through the yard gathering them and eating them right on the spot. She remembered that my cousin, her only son, and I would pretend that the pecans were the spoils of a fierce fictitious battle and that they were the precious loot we had seized from Captain Bly himself.

Calling my thoughts back to the present moment, I sat in my beautiful home, comfortable and safe at my fine kitchen table a thousand miles from those days and those thoughts. I was a grown man now, and the time had passed so quickly. My whole world was different now from when I picked pecans off the fresh-cut grass and popped them in my mouth. I thought about how much had changed around me, but how little I had changed internally. Of course, I was a Christian and that made a huge impact on me, but beyond that, my personality still belonged to that innocent little boy. I had become more guarded perhaps, less trusting and more mature in my focus and drive. But somewhere in the midst of it all, there was still a little knobby-kneed boy who wanted to go outside and play. And as I sat at the kitchen table, I could feel him inside of me — still.

My aunt thought she had sent me a beautiful box of pecans, but what she really sent was a treasure chest full of memories. My cousin is now dead and so are most of the older relatives who composed the cast of my carefree childhood summers. But it seemed like they were all back in my life again as I applied pressure to the first pecan shell and heard it crack. I could hear the crackle of catfish frying and taste the sweet iced tea that wasn't made from an instant mix in a jar. I could hear the laughter of my boisterous relatives telling jokes and having fun; and it felt good and safe, warm and fun. For a moment, I could hear my mother laugh and my father clear his throat. I could inhale the aroma of freshly mowed hay and the sweet smell of my grandmother's farm, where the cow grazed in the fields she had purchased and owned. Yes, my aunt had given me far more than a box of pecans, which, left alone, would have been a gourmet meal for some hungry squirrel. She had reminded me of my essence, my core, my center. My aunt had sent me a sermon in a shell, a friendly reminder to me that it is the little things that matter. Life is really as simple as a pecan. It also has to be shelled, enjoyed, savored, and remembered.

You know, if we are not careful today, we will forget the little things that make life worth living. Happiness is not found in the things we possess. Most of the time, the more we own, the more we have to deal with. The things we possess create more and more responsibilities, and we often become consumed by those responsibilities to the point that we lose the child within us to the adult before us. I have seen us trade sunsets in for laptops, the smell of morning rain for Jacuzzis. I have seen us trade home-cooked meals for Chinese takeout, home-made pot roast for gourmet meals in a bag. And for what, I wonder? Has it added to us or taken from us? I am not sure, but I think we need to take a moment and think about what we want most out of life before our American dream ends up a nightmare.

I am not saying that we shouldn't acquire things. I have worked hard to make life better for my family and to give my children the advantages that were once unthinkable. But I do wonder if we haven't started to think that the more we have, the happier we will be. Maybe, instead of giving my children summer camps, learning labs, and computer gadgets, I should have slipped them a few pecans to provide them with that core that helped me along the way. Sometimes we give everything but what made us who we are.

Maybe the next time you want to give someone something really impressive, you should gather some pecans or send them some homemade jelly. Maybe the most impressive gift under the tree doesn't have to be professionally wrapped or come in the form of an ounce of precious perfume with a name that no one can pronounce but everyone wants to own. Maybe the little things would mean the most to someone you love and know well enough to understand what gives them a memory and sense of well-being.

It isn't always how much you spend that makes a gift exquisite; it can be how much thought you put into finding something that really fit that person and caused them to realize that you know them well enough to see what they are missing. Making a really great impression on that special someone in your life could be as simple as a bag of nuts.

The nuts from my aunt went a long way. Some of them were swallowed nearly whole, others crunched and sprinkled over ice cream. Several of them made it to the top of my wife's cream cheese–filled brownies, and quite a few ended up glazed with syrup, baked at 350 degrees, crowning a delicious pecan pie. But whatever their fate, what was most precious wasn't what I did with them. It was that someone took the time to give me the memories that reminded me that there is something so sweet — and I do mean sweet — about the little things.

11

A Little Child Shall Lead Them

17

A little Child Shall Lead Them

He is like a tornado in footie pajamas. On Christmas morning, he bolts out of his bedroom and thunders down the stairway, full speed ahead until he jerks to a stop just short of crashing into the Christmas tree. He is my youngest son, Dexter, and he has inherited from his mother and me a true passion for Christmas. Or maybe it has something to do with the fact that his arrival was announced on Christmas morning!

We have a Christmas tradition at our house — well, the children call it a "rule." On Christmas morning, everyone must wait in their bedrooms until they hear me bellow an invitation to come to the Christmas tree. I want to check everything out and make sure it is just right — and I want to be ready with the camera when they burst into the living room. The wait is almost unbearable, they say. The older children are more composed now than they were years ago, and they take the delay in stride. I'm so proud of the way they have developed patience and a healthy tolerance for their good ol' Dad!

But, as I've told you, Dexter is a different story. You would think his bedroom is a torture chamber the way he moans and groans to come out on Christmas morning. You would think I was making him wait a hundred years, when really, I try to be ready pretty quickly. When I am, I brace myself for his onslaught. Yes, he leads the pack on the charge to the tree, everyone else following a safe distance behind him, laughing and smiling and shaking their heads over his unbridled excitement.

Most of us in the family are at the point where we comment appropriately about how beautifully our packages are wrapped, and we maintain an element of dignity as we open them. Again, not Dexter; that boy tears into his gifts with such zeal that I am afraid he may destroy the gift before he ever finds out what it is! But do you know something? The rest of us do pick up on his enthusiasm. He raises the joy level in our living room like no one else could. Why? Just because he's still a child. His age is still in the single digits, and there's something about his age and his lack of experience with the difficulties of life that gives him an enormous capacity for happiness and enables him to maximize every moment. With his youth — as with youth in general — comes such innocence, such purity, such intensity. He is the ringmaster of Christmas at our house, and he leads the rest of us to the most incredible places of fun and celebration and all-out wonder as together we sit around the Christmas tree.

When I think about Dexter and the delight he is to our lives, my thoughts can't help but wander toward the phrase in the Bible that says "and a little child shall lead them" (Isaiah 11:6).

The little Child who began to lead us under the star at the stable grew to be a toddler and a school-age boy and a twelve-year-old, who got separated from his parents in a crowd. He grew to be a teenager and a young adult, and He completed His assignment on earth by age thirty-three. One of these days, He will return to earth with the blast of a trumpet to call home His own. So, He did not remain a child, but His purity is just like a child's. The joy that rings in His heart is unpolluted and uncorrupted, just like a child's. He overlooks our faults, always sees the best in us, and loves unconditionally — just like a child.

I love to think about Jesus' coming to earth as a baby. And every Christmas, in our church I sing about it. By now, this song is such a tradition that there might be a protest in the parking lot if I didn't sing it. It's called "Little Boy, My Hope's on You."

Isn't it amazing that I can sing about putting my hope in a little boy? What a wonder that God would come to earth as a child. Just think: He who owns the universe was born in a barn, lay in a manger, and had mere lowly animals witness His entry into the world. He could have had angels cover the tops of volcanoes and then have warmed Himself by the glowing embers of their sacrifice. He could have hailed the wind from a distant tornado and been ushered in its whirl into some ancient metropolis. Or perhaps He could have set His majestic feet on the peaks of some snow-covered alp, some spiraling mountain slope, and drunk the nectar of heaven while angelic hosts serenaded Him with an aria. He could have had a grand processional, an event that would be proper and fitting for a royal ambassador sent to the foreign soil of this planet to bear the most significant message we would ever hear. He could have come with royal documentation that authenticated His high and regal position and graceful deity. But He purposefully avoided the pageantry that was his rightful due, and He came into a dusty, dank, rodent-filled place where no human would desire to abide. Just a little boy making His first earthly appearance in the starlit night of a backyard barn.

What a sharp contrast to the first man, Adam, who came into the world fully grown, married, and employed in no time at all. That was not the case with the last man Adam (otherwise known as Jesus). He came so humbly, even more so than I have described, and ended up wrapped in swaddling rags that had been lying around in a stable! No pomp, no ceremony, no ritual — just unbridled, unfeigned love for this world.

I have often wondered, since God proved to us in Adam that He can have a son who bypassed childhood, why did He come to redeem us in the small, frail package of an infant?

I can only imagine that He appreciates, as I do, the unique innocence and fresh love that emanates from the face of a child, a child who is so obviously pure from this world's constant contaminating influence. A child leaks love through the pores of his skin. His outstretched arms offer acceptance without any bias or bigotry. His gentle cooing at the end of a feeding teaches our souls to rest in the comfort of divine provision. And his rest on the breast of his mother exhibits his grace to trust so perfectly.

In the same way that a baby trusts his mother not to drop him but to sustain him, we now trust the Savior, the Lord Jesus, to keep us, bless us, and protect us. He comes to us as God's strength wrapped in human weakness. But like all Christmas gifts, the content is far more exquisite than the wrapping it comes in. Personally, He is the Gift I can't wait to unwrap moment by moment and day by day. After all these years, I am still unfolding the grace and majesty encompassed in His wondrous redemption.

I suspect you have lived long enough by now to have learned a little bit about where you can and cannot put your hope. You may have learned the hard way that you cannot put your hope in a savings account or a stock portfolio, because though that may leave your wallet full, it may also leave your soul bankrupt. You may have learned that you cannot put your hope in that job or that promotion you worked so hard to get, because though that may gain you professional prestige, it may cost you the ones you love. You may have learned that you cannot put your hope in a romantic relationship, because though that may leave your head spinning with delight, it may also leave your heart empty or broken if you have not chosen wisely.

As I have counseled countless wounded, aching, frustrated people over the years, I cannot even tell you how many broken hearts and broken homes are the result of misplaced hope. Sometimes the bottom line to a whole heap of trouble is that someone put hope in something that couldn't deliver. There isn't a human being alive who won't fail you somehow, some way. There isn't a material possession or an earthly endeavor that is able to come through for you 100 percent of the time.

No, my friend, only Jesus holds our hope. The hope in our hearts is a precious commodity, and only Jesus is worth investing it in. Do you know something? I have a wish for you this Christmas. I wish that you will come to know, or know more deeply, the little Boy I've put my hope in. If life has robbed you of hope, I am asking you to dare to hope again. If you have been so disappointed that you have determined not to hope again (because then you won't hurt again), would you be willing to try just one more time? A little Child is leading you — and I promise, as long as you hope in Him, you will not be let down. Come on, look up, beyond the night sky where the stars are twinkling, look toward heaven and breathe that wonderful declaration with me: "Little Boy, my hope's on you."

12

God's Timing Is Perfect

Would you do something for me? Put your fingers in your ears, closing them tight enough for you to hear your own heartbeat. Are you listening to the *thump, thump, thump?* That's the rhythm of your life. Well, to be more accurate, that's the rhythm of your physical life. There is an entirely different beat for your spiritual life, and God is the one who sets the tempo. Not only does He have a plan for your life that He backs up with promises from His word, He also has specific times and seasons for advancing His purpose for you.

Occasionally, something will happen suddenly and you will think God has moved very quickly in your life. You may even be surprised by what He does. But more often than not, He starts early, preparing your heart for the changes He wants to make. Usually, He will begin to loosen your grip on a particular situation — a job in which you have felt secure, the place where you live, maybe even a relationship. He often begins to put dreams or ideas or new interests inside of you, and you begin to have a passion to pursue them. *But wait*, you think, *I cannot see those dreams fulfilled or those ideas executed or those interests developed in the place where I am!* And there you have it: The desire for change has taken root in you.

Then the wait begins. There is often quite a lapse between the desire for change and its fulfillment. Why? Because the timing must be right in order for the change to have its maximum benefit. Many times, God wants to heal some painful memory from your past so that it will not pollute your future. Sometimes He wants to teach you how to have better relationships because He wants to give you one that will last until you take your last breath. He may want to expand your knowledge so that you are able to get a job that requires more skill and offers more pay. Or He may want to develop your character so that He can enlarge your influence.

There are all sorts of reasons for the wait, but you must remember that His timing is perfect. He never misses a beat, never acts prematurely, never has to play catch-up because He was late. You may not realize just how perfect His divine cadence is until after the dust has settled, but I guarantee that when you allow Him to work His plan in His timing, you will marvel at the perfection of His plan.

I beg you, whatever you do, do not fall out of step with God's timing for your life. Seek to understand His seasons for you and get your heart tuned in to that heavenly beat; then march. You see, it is easier to know when to move and when not to when you can hear a beat. Anybody with any sense of rhythm at all will feel awkward trying to march in a way that is not in sync with the beat — in fact, it's almost impossible! Because they've "got" the rhythm, they know instinctively when to make the next move. Nothing else feels right.

So it is with the timing of God. When you are walking to His beat, trying to rush ahead or fall behind just doesn't feel right. You will often know when you are in a season of change. Just as the appearance of Christmas tree lots and decorations indicate that Christmas is coming, something in your heart will let you know that change is in store. When you enter the season, listen carefully for the beat so that you will fall right in line with God's perfect timing. You may have to plug your ears against the clamor of the world or the voices of well-meaning friends, but getting quiet enough to connect with your soul is worth it. Only then can you hear that *thump, thump, thump.*

Speaking of seasons, my wife loves Christmastime. That just happens to be her favorite season of the year. I am not talking about a casual affection, nor do I mean that she enjoys the season more than most people seem to. No, she goes *all out.* This tremendous lady fills our home with Christmas music before Thanksgiving. Sometimes Bing Crosby and Nat King Cole and the London Philharmonic are all competing from different CD players. It would not be uncommon to walk through our house and hear something like, "Hark! The herald angels we have heard on high, sweetly dreaming of a white Christmas on a midnight clear . . ."

Yes, when the holiday season approaches, the woman I love sets out on a mission like a race-car driver speeding toward the finish line, leaving a spray of dust in her wake. She fully intends, every year, to totally transform the place where we live — and she does. She has so many flashing, blinking, singing, dancing decorations that I just cross my fingers and hope we will not blow the whole neighborhood electrical circuit! And after a long, busy day, if I cannot find my recliner, I have learned to assume it has been replaced by a Christmas tree and will reappear when the new year gets underway.

But if you catch my wife in a quiet moment and ask her what she likes about Christmas, she will inevitably begin to talk about its timing. She loves the rhythm of the year and the fact that Christmas is not like Labor Day or Memorial Day or even Easter because the dates of those holidays vary from one year to the next. Not Christmas. Ready or not, Christmas morning dawns on December 25 year after year after year. You will not hear anyone waiting in line at the grocery store say, "Everything is out of whack this year because Christmas is late," or "Well, Christmas is early this year, so we will have to wait a long time for New Year's." My wife appreciates the dependability of the timing of Christmas, as regular as a downbeat, and she both understands its season and revels in its one-day crescendo.

Lest my wife take issue with me, I will confess that I also contribute to the happy Christmas chaos. You see, I am almost as happy in the kitchen as I am in the pulpit. Give me some eggs and sugar and spices and measuring cups and mixing bowls and I will go to town! Whether it's cakes or casseroles or corn pudding, I'm the man at our house.

The lessons of timing are important when

I cook. For instance, if I don't beat the meringue long enough, I will end up with sticky, gooey egg whites that are no good for anything. If I do not allow the oven time to heat properly, I will not get my desired result even if I leave my well-prepared dish in for the right length of time. And if I do wait for the oven to preheat and then fail to remove that carrot cake at the right moment, well, then I have nothing but a burned, blackened semisweet mess that would have been fabulous had I only paid attention to the timing and removed it when I was supposed to. After years of experience, I can find my rhythm in the kitchen and march to the beat pretty well. (Once you've charred a few carrot cakes, you start to listen pretty closely.) I can work on several recipes simultaneously, because I have a sense of how long each step of the process will take. I find my groove and get in it, and the results, if I do say so myself, are usually quite delicious!

Learning timing is a process, and it takes all of us awhile. It is sort of like baking a great cake and developing the art of doing it just right and knowing when it is perfectly done. It's also like preparing a big meal and developing the skills needed to prepare multiple dishes and then learning what to do when so that they can all be delivered to the table piping hot. We often host our entire family for dinner at our house, and have fed thirty people or more — all at the same time. Believe me, our kitchen is not set up for that kind of production! In order to get everything ready on time and on the table at the proper temperature, we have to use crock pots, roasters, chafing dishes, microwaves, and everything else to pull it off.

But as it is with dinner, so it is with life. You have to know that even if you do not have everything you think you need, everything has a way of turning out all right. God is an expert at timing; He has His timing down pat, and He knows exactly when to bless you with what. Maybe you are caught up in thinking, *Well, this is not going to be ready in my life* and *That is not going to be ready in time for this. . . .* Shhhhhhhhh. Be still and relax. A Master Chef is serving you and His name is Jesus. My timing may not be perfect and I may serve something that isn't hot enough, but not Jesus. He knows when and how to do what. Trust Him. He will be sure that everything is in place in your life and waiting for you. It will be the perfect temperature and the perfect time.

You know, the Bible says a lot about God, but I cannot find one verse that says He was ever late. Not one. He will not be late in your life, nor will He allow you to be late for anything He has for you. He is marching to the beat of His own heart. I challenge you to hear it, to get in step with it. I guarantee you that His timing in your life is absolutely perfect. *Thump. Thump. Thump.* Thump . . .

13

Don't Wait Too Late

I once worked in a department store during the Christmas season and, as happens to most people who are employed in the retail industry, I had to work on Christmas Eve. I had heard about so-called last-minute shoppers, but until that year, I did not fully appreciate this unique group of people! I could hardly believe it as I watched this holiday phenomenon unfold before my very eyes.

The sequence of events was remarkably similar for every last-minute shopper who came to our store. We could almost hear them coming, like a train roaring down a railroad track. They jerked to a halt outside the entrance and swung open the doors with such vigor that it's a wonder they stayed on their hinges. Most last-minute shoppers either collided with part of the door frame or at least bumped into the wall as they tried to get into our establishment. They all looked about the same, wearing snow-covered boots and cloaked in heavy coats, warm hats, and a general air of total chaos.

Their mad dash to the store left their faces flushed and their heads bobbing as they struggled to catch their breath. Most of them had the most remarkable ability to spot a sales associate quickly. They would zero in on one of us and, while making their approach, would pull out a soggy Christmas list, a crumpled scrap of paper from a purse or a pocket, and say between heaves, "Uh, do you have a [desired item] in [such-and-such a color] size [whatever]? I just have to have it for [so-and-so] and it's all she wants for Christmas and she's been talking about it since Memorial Day and she'll be devastated if she doesn't get it . . ."

Some sales associates joined the frenzy and darted around the store on a mission to find that perfect gift and satisfy the customer. I suppose those were the clerks with the spiritual gift of mercy! More often than not, when the search was over, all they could say to the panic-ridden customer was, "I'm sorry, sir. The Big Wheels are all gone" or, "Ma'am, I wish we did have that dress in a size 6, but all we have is a 4 and a 10." Responses like that were as common as the slush in the parking lot, and when we uttered such statements, we meant them. If we said we didn't have it, we didn't have it. Nevertheless, at that point, some customers seemed to believe that we could make the item they needed appear out of thin air if they asked in a louder voice. Others thought perhaps we could pull one out of a hat if they resorted to tears and whining. It never worked. Nine times out of ten, they wanted an item we *had* stocked, something they could have easily purchased if they had visited the store three weeks earlier. Those popular Christmas gifts simply were not available at 5:49 p.m. on the night before Christmas, when we closed at 6:00.

Now wait a minute. Hold everything. Let's rewind our story just a little bit. Do you mean to tell me that little Suzy has been telling her mother since Memorial Day that she wanted that one-and-only special baby doll? Do you mean that little Johnny started talking to his dad about that racetrack all the way back in the merry month of May? And these parents are just starting to shop for it now? It didn't take me long behind the department store cash register to realize that these poor souls were the sad victims of waiting too long to go after what they knew they needed to buy. And their friends and relatives would end up as victims as well and be disappointed on Christmas morning because someone waited too long to go shopping.

As I think about the tardy gift-givers, I realize that last-minute desperation is not unique to Christmas shoppers, and that if there is anything good about having observed them, it is the life lesson they can teach us. How many times do you and I sit back and wait until the last minute to institute changes we should have made last week, last month, last year? How many times do we know what we need or want to do, and then let time pass us by until it's too late?

There's a story in the Bible about some "last-minute shoppers." Now this was long before Big Wheels were invented. These people were not even out in the market looking for a specific type of cow or donkey. In fact, if the truth be told, they weren't really shopping at all, but they did have a desperate need and time had run out. Maybe you know their names — Mary and Martha. Maybe you remember that Martha was the type-A, the workaholic, the one who wanted to make sure everything was just perfect that night when Jesus came to dinner. Mary, on the other hand, was the relaxed one, the one who let pressure roll off of her like water off a duck's back, the one who was happiest sitting at Jesus' feet listening to His stories and advice. She didn't even know the roast was capable of burning, while Martha flew around that kitchen trying to make salad, set the table, put wine in the glasses, and light the candles all at the same time!

But this unlikely pair, as different as they were, came together in grief when their beloved brother Lazarus was dying. Once they realized he would not be with them much longer, they sent Jesus an urgent message: "Lord, behold, he whom you love is sick" (John 11:3). I can imagine, in modern English, that Martha might have said, "Get over here this minute!" while Mary would have pleaded, "Please hurry, Jesus. I know you're busy, but this is an emergency. Please come as fast as you can!"

Now, understand that Lazarus was one of Jesus' closest friends. The Bible says that "Jesus loved Martha and her sister and Lazarus" (John 11:5). But do you know what He did when He found out that Lazarus was dying? He did not drop everything and rush to Lazarus' bedside but stayed right where He was for two whole days. By the time He arrived in the town where Lazarus lived, poor Lazarus had been in a tomb for four days! When they saw Jesus, Martha complained, "Lord, if you had been here, my brother would not have died" (John 11:21).

I never question Jesus because His timing is perfect. He knew Lazarus was dead, and He delayed His visit to the sisters so that He might do the miracle of raising him back to life. But I do question Martha. I wonder why she was so quick to blame Jesus and why she did not say to Him instead, "If only we had sent for you sooner, then we might still have our brother today."

There's a little bit of Martha in most of us. We can point our fingers so quickly and blame others instead of standing up and taking responsibility for our actions. I wonder why it is that we are so slow to go after what we need or want. Often we are afraid. Many times the risk seems too great. Sometimes we don't want to take the chance because we don't want to fail. Sometimes it feels safer to cradle our dreams in the privacy of our own minds than to pursue them in front of people who might laugh or criticize us.

But I have good news. The same Jesus who gave Lazarus back to his sisters alive and well is in business today. He is the one who gives courage to act. He is the safety net under that tightrope of risk you may be afraid to take. He isn't finished doing miracles, and, in fact, He may be waiting on you to do something so that He can work a sign and a wonder.

I want to challenge you today, on the brink of a brand-new year, to dig deep within your heart and unearth those things you know you need to do. I want you to take those things and swat the dirt off of them and look at them and determine that they will not go undone any longer. The Spirit of God — the Spirit of Jesus, the Lazarus-raiser — is a spirit of power. He empowers you to do the things you have not yet done. Call on His might, get off the dime, and get with the program He's called you to! Live a proactive, on-the-ball life and maximize every moment that you grace the face of this earth. Don't wait too late.

Now, you know that I am a pastor. I love to challenge, but I also love to comfort. Your words of comfort today are this: Lazarus died. Mary and Martha honestly believed that Jesus was late. I want to remind you that He is never late. Even when you honestly believe that something in your life is dead forever, He can come in and raise it up with just a word. You mustn't wallow in regret over that which you think is unredeemable. Jesus is not only a miracle-worker but a Redeemer, and even missed opportunities have a way of getting woven into the fabric of your life in a redemptive way. Jesus is a Restorer, and as long as you are living in Him, it is never too late.

14

God Always Has a Plan

It was a bone-chilling West Virginia winter, and every gentle snowflake announced the Yuletide season. White blankets of snow shrouded the mountains and wrapped the world in peace. Downtown streets shimmered and sparkled with colored lights and ribbons and bows. Even the streetlights were dressed in their holiday best and seemed to sing out "Fa-la-la-la-la!" Happy people hustled in and out of the stores with their Christmas treasures, while children could hardly contain themselves as the excitement of the season threatened to consume them!

Not so at our house. At the Jakes residence, the peeling paint hung from the house like icicles. The snow failed to cover the sagging gables and leaking gutters. While every passing day filled the hearts of so many with joyful anticipation, the rapidly approaching Christmas morning brought nothing but anxiety to me.

I was afraid there would be no Christmas for us. The Union Carbide plant where I worked had been shut down and my job was eliminated. By December, the unemployment had run out and we were struggling — stretched to the breaking point by the demands of everyday existence. No matter how hard we tried to make ends meet, there always seemed to be a big space between them! While other living rooms had turned their attention to Christmas trees bedecked with tinsel and ornaments, ours looked just like it always did — nothing new, nothing different, nothing with branches on which to hang a popcorn chain, nothing to crown with a tinfoil star. While other homes glowed with the glimmer of lights hanging from roofs and windows, our battered front porch was only illuminated by the glare of the bare, yellow bug light dangling from the ceiling.

But Christmas has both its trappings and its gifts. I could live with the fact that our house looked no different during Christmas than it did in the middle of June, except for the snow. I could even live with the absence of a fir tree or a pine. But I could hardly bear the thought that there were no gifts. We did not have money to provide anything for anyone to unwrap on Christmas morning. But God had a plan.

When Christmas morning dawned, I had

a sick feeling in my stomach. Even though the twin boys were very young, they were old enough to know what Christmas was. It broke my heart to know that I could not fill their little hands with Christmas presents and that I had nothing to give my wife. I remembered our first Christmas together.

I knew she was the one for me. Oh yes, indeed, she was the woman I wanted to marry. And since I was so madly in love with her (and I think she liked me too!), I asked my mother if we could invite her to Christmas dinner. We invited her lovely mother as well, and I was thrilled when they accepted. Just having her by my side during the meal was Christmas gift enough for me. In fact, I was so enamored that I hardly noticed that she and her mother were — well, they were of a different temperament from most of my family. While we tended to be gregarious, they were more reserved. While we thought nothing of laughter and high-energy festivities, they were the kind of gracious women who covered their mouths with their napkins as they giggled politely. It takes all kinds, though, and by the end of the meal, I could tell that the two families, as different as we were, would get along just fine.

When it was time to open gifts, I presented my wife-to-be with a gift I had chosen especially for her. It was an outfit — not just any outfit, but the most beautiful outfit I could find, complete with a sweater and a shawl. I knew when she opened it that it was a hit. She loved it; she thought I was great! And I must admit, I was quite proud of it myself!

On that happy day, I never dreamed there would be a Christmas when I would not be able to give her something as wonderful as that outfit. We never expected to be in the situation we were in. But we were. I longed for happier days — even if they only existed in my memory.

My recollections were interrupted by a knock on the door. I rose to open it and saw my mother-in-law standing on the porch. I still don't know how she did it, but she showed up that morning with gifts for everyone. I am not talking about a few small favors; I am talking about tricycles for the boys, groceries for Christmas dinner and everything! It was wonderful!

Looking back, I know my mother-in-law did not wake up on Christmas morning and decide to bring us a carload of presents. She couldn't have — stores weren't open on Christmas Day. No, she had planned this surprise well in advance for us. She had known that Christmas was coming, and it did not sneak up on her any more than it sneaks up on the rest of us.

Nothing sneaks up on God either. Just as He did for our family that Christmas, He always has a plan. He did not panic when Eve handed Adam the apple. He did not wonder what to do when He gazed from heaven down upon the whole earth and saw sin so repulsive that nothing short of a worldwide flood would cleanse it. He did not gasp in shock and horror when the filth and degradation of Sodom and Gomorrah caught His eye. He didn't even worry when Jonah ended up in a whale's stomach because that seemed better than obeying God.

No, from the beginning, before time ever was, God had a plan. He had a plan to populate the earth with people who would love Him and people who would not. He had a plan for times and seasons, for men and women, for families and friendships, for kings and kingdoms. He had a plan to break into history at one crucial moment in a little town called Bethlehem. He had a plan to crush the head of the enemy and secure victory on earth and in heaven for all who will call upon His name. And He has a plan for you — an intricate, personal, perfectly timed, well-oiled plan so dripping with goodness that it would blow your mind if you really understood it.

Sometimes it is invisible to your natural eyes; sometimes even the eyes of your heart cannot perceive it. Sometimes you will want to ask God if He knows where you are; sometimes you may wish He didn't. But you never stop living smack in the middle of His unfolding purpose. Like a meticulous architect who marks the spaces for even the electrical outlets, God has drawn a plan for your life down to the last detail, and He is watching over it, guiding you this way and that, saying to you, "Turn here." "Stop there." "Now, full speed ahead and don't quit until you cross the finish line!"

The infinite eyes of God roam the earth choosing friends for you, finding jobs for you, connecting you with opportunities to discover and express your passions and your gifts. If you are single, He is keeping tabs on that husband or wife He is holding just for you until the moment is perfect for two to become one. He is teaching you today the lessons you will need tomorrow. He orders your steps, making sure you are in the right place at the right time to accomplish what is in His heart for you. Not only this, but if you read Zephaniah 3:17 in its original Hebrew, you will see that He is so excited over you that He can hardly contain Himself, singing and dancing and spinning around, celebrating who you are and all that He wants you to be and do and enjoy. All you have to do is follow the Star. He knows exactly where you're going and how much you will love it when you get there.

No one follows perfectly; no one gets it right all the time. When you stumble, or even when you fall flat on your face, the point is not how bruised you are or how loud you scream. The point is that you get up. Even if you must limp for a while, limp with grace. Limp with style, limp with gumption; just keep looking upward and walk on.

There will be moments, too, when you feel you are walking well, when you are not tripping over your own feet, but you find yourself face-to-face with trial or tragedy. I want to remind you: When trouble knocks on the door of your house or on the door of your heart, God has a plan. Struggle may show up on your doorstep as the police officer with a solemn look on his face, the look that signals the worst kind of news. It may come back home as the prodigal child who's out of money and into drugs. Devastation may arrive as a diagnosis you never thought your own ears would hear. It may take the form of a spouse who doesn't love you anymore or a layoff or financial setback so severe that you will have to sell the house.

Whatever the crisis that seems uniquely designed to produce your downfall, God has a plan. Your challenge is to remember — no matter what happens — that God has a plan. And God is as good as His Word, which says this about you: "For I know the plans I have for you, declares the Lord, plans to prosper you and not to harm you, plans to give you a hope and a future" (Jeremiah 29:11, NIV). I have known my share of struggle and of heartbreak. Sometimes it has been hard to see God's plan through the pain, but He has never failed. Not once.

I can say to you with authority that comes from personal experience that out of your disappointments will come divine appointments. Out of your most costly mistakes will come your most priceless gems of wisdom. Out of your bruised and bleeding places will come your greatest strength. Out of your haunting fears will come a holy faith — if you will determine to believe that God has a plan for you, that He wants to give you a good future, filled with hope, and that He will bring His purposes to pass in your life in ways that are likely to astound you.

15

God Works with Wood

Mary gets a lot of attention around Christmastime. People sing about her, read her story in Luke and Matthew, think about how difficult that donkey ride must have been for someone nine months pregnant. Most years, she even gets her picture on a postage stamp. Now I believe this chosen woman deserves a place of honor in the hearts and minds of everyone who knows Jesus, and I know that she was a very special young lady. She was the only human being to share her life and breath and blood with the Son of God as she carried Him in her womb.

But although she alone nourished Him and labored with Him and gave Him birth, she did have someone beside her. His name was Joseph, and beyond that, we really don't know too much about him. We know that he was an honorable man, and that when he heard Mary was pregnant and knew her child was not his, he determined to leave her quietly, without making a scene, and to cause her as little embarrassment as possible. We know that he was a descendent of King David, and that he paid his taxes (that was the reason for the trip to Bethlehem!). We know that he stayed faithfully by Mary's side, even though he had good reason to be more nervous than most fathers-to-be — imagine you were charged with being the earthly father to the Son of God. We know that he was the kind of man God trusted enough to speak to and that every time the Lord visited him in a dream, he obeyed the divine directive. Finally, we know what he did for a living. He was a carpenter.

I can imagine his carpenter's shop: the tools of his trade neatly arranged as they hung from the wall and the smell of fresh-cut timber filling the air. I'm sure his work-table was often blanketed in wood shavings by the end of the day, and that a few stray nails had rolled under the table or into a corner of the dusty floor from time to time. I would guess that the creative side of his brain envisioned the beauty of the crafts that would bear his name, while the technical side figured out how to make them most functional and efficient. Judging from his behavior as the Bible records it, I would say he was a man of excellence not only in character but in his chosen profession.

Other than that, I can relate to Joseph and his trade only slightly. When I was in junior high school, I took a shop class. The goal of the class was to be able to make a set of wooden bookends we could take home to our mothers — bookends she wouldn't want to hide on the top shelf of a closet! After cutting and sanding, I succeeded in creating a pair of functional, albeit slightly lopsided, bookends that my mother proudly displayed in our living room.

In biblical times, there were no shop classes. Young men learned their trades from their fathers. Because Joseph was a carpenter, Jesus would have been expected to follow in his footsteps and earn a living as a carpenter too. We can't learn very much about Jesus' childhood from the stories in the Bible. We do know one verse that is so familiar to many of us: "Jesus increased in wisdom and stature, and in favor with God and man" (Luke 2:52). That is wonderful, but it doesn't give us any clues about the specifics of His everyday life as he grew up in Nazareth. Luke's gospel does include a story that the others do not, and I think it reveals that Jesus wasn't exactly cut out to stand in a shop all day and swing a hammer!

Mary and Joseph journeyed to Jerusalem every year during the Passover feast, and when Jesus was twelve years old, He made the trip with them. In those days, parents did not have to watch their children as carefully as they do today, so Jesus was allowed to mingle through the crowd with which His family traveled. After the feast concluded and the Passover pilgrims headed home, Mary and Joseph realized that they had not seen Jesus since they began their journey back to Nazareth. After three days, they finally located Him in the temple in Jerusalem, talking with the religious scholars and amazing them with His knowledge and understanding.

When Mary asked, essentially, "What in the world are you doing?" He responded to her with this question: "Did you not know that I must be about my Father's business?" (Luke 2:49). I wonder if that was their first indication that Jesus would perhaps choose a religious vocation rather than the carpenter's trade. Then again, maybe they knew all along.

Joseph wasn't really Jesus' father anyway, and Jesus did not come to earth to make bookends. He is the beginning and the ending of all things and He is the one in whom all things hold together, but He did not make His appearance on earth so that He could give Mary a home accessory!

Now I suspect you know very well what carpenters do: They make things and they fix things. They do so with a marvelous blend of artistry and skill. A carpenter tends to be exact, and all self-respecting carpenters strive to make their work as near perfect as possible. That's exactly what Jesus does, so perhaps He is more of a carpenter than I thought!

Here is my question for you today: What do you need Him to make or to fix in your life? Do you need Him to create a fresh desire in your heart for your spouse or for more patience with your children? Do you need Him to mend that place in you that has been hurting so deeply for so long? Do you need Him to make an opportunity for you, when every door before you seems nailed shut? Do you need Him to fix some of your attitudes? Do you need Him to heal your physical body or restore a broken relationship?

I have never seen a project He could not tackle with grace and style and perfection. I have never seen Him create anything that is not breathtakingly beautiful, or known Him to fix anything that does not end up working better than it did before. That's just how He is. He is a master craftsman. But the medium in which He works just happens to be the hearts of broken humanity.

But now that I think about it, I am struck by the fact that so much of His ministry did involve wood. He was born in a wooden stable and He rested in a wooden manger; He was raised as the son of a woodworker; and He died on a wooden Cross. He started His wood project in Bethlehem, and completed it at Calvary. With His own body nailed to the rugged beams of the Cross, He uttered the words that changed the lives of everyone who would live from that day forward: "It is finished." With that, He made possible a life of joy and peace and strength and wholeness for you and for me.

Given the fact that Jesus' most significant earthly moments involved wood, I suppose it is no wonder that we celebrate Christmas by bringing trees into our homes. But I fear we have departed from the profound and simple meaning of His trees as we have sought to make Christmas bigger and brighter. I mean, can you believe how many different kinds of Christmas trees there are these days? There are silk trees and plastic trees, aluminum trees and flocked trees, gold-sprayed trees and just good old fresh-cut pine and fir trees. There are trees that feature nothing but angels, some that celebrate the joys of fishing, some that carry out a Mardi Gras theme, some that are adorned with antique ornaments from a certain era, some with nothing but shiny glass balls hanging off of them, and there are monochromatic trees. Then there are the trees that tell the story of your life or your family's life through the decorations that are lovingly unpacked year after year. Those are the kind of decorations not valued for their beauty or their contribution to a particular theme but for the memories they hold.

I don't know what kind of tree you'll have this year, but I do know that you won't find a Christmas tree in the biblical account of Jesus' birth. I suppose if there is any spiritual significance at all to the evergreen boughs that grace our homes during the holidays, maybe it is that God wants us to see the wood and remember everything He's done for us. As you set up your tree and decorate it and hopefully spend some quiet moments watching its lights twinkle, would you please remember Jesus? You've heard it said before, but He really is the reason for the season.

16

Let It Go

Whether or not you believe in the jolly old fellow in the red suit, you've no doubt seen his picture. I'm sure you are familiar with the one in which he is smiling just as big as you please, with his eyes all atwinkle and a grin on his face that would stretch from here to Omaha — the one where his enormous sack of toys and gifts is slung over his shoulder and he does not seem to be burdened in the least by the weight or the bulk of it.

You know by now that that man is not real. But do you know something else? I don't think that bag on his back ever had anything in it, because nobody who runs around with that kind of a load has a sparkle in his eye. Oh, he may be able to fake the smile or to pinch his cheeks to make them rosy, but the sparkle — not a chance.

Perhaps you have observed, as I have, that the picture-perfect Santa Claus is not the only person who carries an enormous pack from place to place. No, people everywhere struggle to walk under the weight of baggage on their backs — it's just that theirs is not too obvious and they would never dream of posing for a picture with it. If you were to stop such a person and peek inside her sack, you would probably be staring straight into her past, looking right down the line of her entire life. And oh, the sights you would see. You might see guilt over an abortion or consuming remorse over some kind of costly business mistake. You might see the pain of divorce or the disappointment of not being able to go to college. You might see the black hole of loneliness or rejection. You might see abuse or abandonment, brokenness or bitterness, unforgiveness or insecurity. And those are only some of the things that get packed in the suitcases of the past and carried around for years.

More people than I can count have walked into my office dragging heavy loads. I have helped unpack many a bag, and I have been there to assist like a little elf as a person's past was pulled out into the light of day, one painful piece at a time. I have seen how crushing and crippling the weight of the past can be to people.

I do understand many of the reasons we feel we must hold on to the past like carry-on baggage. We have such fear of the unknown, and often, human nature compels us to stay in a bad relationship because we are not sure we can handle being alone. We fear becoming strong and confident, because we are experts at being weak and dependent! We know that we are masters at being unhealthy, and we don't know if we can or will be equally good at being healthy! We continue old thoughts or habits or activities because they are familiar to us — at least we know what we are dealing with. We become so comfortable with the familiar that we sink into it, moment by moment, like a tired working man falls into his easy chair at the end of a long day. We fail to realize that the familiar can be fatal.

Nevertheless, I have only two words of advice concerning your past: *Let go.* As long as you carry it with you, it will get heavier and heavier. It will haunt you and taunt you and keep you from enjoying the present and from being able to gladly anticipate the future. It can keep you from trying things you need to try, because it will remind you how many times you have failed. It can keep you from reaching out to a new friend, because an old one betrayed you. It can keep you from going back to school, because you were not able to finish the first time. It can keep you from saying "yes" to that nice man who asks you out for dinner, because so many men have hurt you in the past.

As long as you hold on to the past, it will influence you and it will steal your life — one opportunity at a time. There is only one way to render the past powerless and that is to *let it go*. You will have to decide for yourself how you want to let it go. Some people can read a book like this one and let go easily once they realize how much damage the past is inflicting. Some may need to get out a piece of paper, write down every painful memory, and burn it. Some may need to write "past" on a rock and hurl it into the nearest river. Some may need to visit with a pastor or a counselor or a trusted friend and talk things out until everything is released. It doesn't matter how you let the past go — just do it.

There is only one person who can enable you to release your past, and He is the One we celebrate this season. He is not the robust image of the man with the white fur collar; He is the most real being ever to walk the earth — Jesus Christ. My wife and I never taught our children to believe in Santa Claus. We weren't spoilsports or Scrooges; we were just so thoroughly thankful for Jesus and the wonderful ways He had changed our lives that we were not willing to turn our focus away from Him for a second

— not even long enough for the shutter to click for a mall photograph! We have encountered His power to heal us and help us and restore our hope. He has brought us out of the past into a place where we fully enjoy the present and look forward to the future, and I know that what He has done for us He longs to do for you.

I submit to you today that His coming brought closure to an entire era of human history. Older forms of worship, older traditions, older offerings, scapegoats, and burning lambs were all abolished with His coming. He fulfilled the law and made possible a life of complete freedom and grace for everyone who would believe in Him. Isn't *that* good news?

It's great news, but not everyone recognized the benefit of His presence while He walked the earth. You see, some people had difficulty letting go of the past. Some preferred to maintain the religious traditions of their ancestors — bound by law and ceremony — rather than to relax in the love of God and enjoy the presence of Jesus in their midst. They were so set in their older traditions, so set in their ideas, that because Jesus didn't fit into the mold they were expecting, they didn't recognize Him. Their fierce grip on the past caused some to miss out on the best thing that could have ever happened to them.

I don't want that to happen to you. I do not want the past to rob you of your present or your future. I'm asking you to think about the end of this year the way a business owner or an accountant does. While others focus their thoughts on how best to celebrate on New Year's Eve, these people hear the clock ticking as loudly as a sonic boom as they scramble to balance their books, search for receipts, amend contracts, issue checks, and request payment from those who owe them money. They know that anything left undone at midnight on December 31 will not be credited to the year that is ending, and bringing closure to as many matters as humanly possible becomes urgent so that the company will finish strong.

As you come to the end of this year, there may be some personal matters to which you need to bring closure. You may want to put a period at the end of a sentence (or a chapter!) of your life. Following the Star means letting go of the past. I tell you, He is the God of new beginnings, and you will not be able to hold anything new if your fists are tightly clenched around something old.

I really want you to enter into the new

year with a lightness in your step — a lightness that comes from the fact that you no longer carry the baggage of your past. I want you to be free to skip and jump and play in the new things that are ahead the way a little child does in a sprinkler on a summer day. I want you to be able to stand tall and face the future with a grin that outshines the smile on any Santa's face. What's that I see? Ah, good. It's that twinkle returning to your eyes as you let go of the past. Keep up the good work. The best way to behold the future is through eyes that have been shut on the past. That way, they will sparkle and dance with anticipation for the bright and wonderful days ahead.

17

Back to the Future

Several years ago, a movie about an old inventor and a curious young man played in theaters all across the United States. It was called *Back to the Future*, and in it the young man travels back through time to visit the town where he lives years before he was born. Have you ever wondered how a person could go back to the future? Well, I've decided that's exactly what most of us do, starting, oh, sometimes as early as the day after Christmas!

Similar scenes seem to play out in living rooms and family rooms across the country. Wads of wrapping paper are piled on the floor, price tags that have been cut off new clothes (because yes, they did fit) are strewn around the room. Open packages that once housed batteries are sitting on the sofa. Perhaps there is even a streamer of ribbon hanging from a light fixture. Children are somewhat content playing with the gifts they've received, while the grown-ups have neatly stacked theirs in boxes because they had to start cooking or cleaning or loading the car for a trip to Grandma's house. Inevitably, someone has something that is the wrong color or the wrong size or for some reason, just won't work.

"It's okay," says Mom. "We can exchange it tomorrow when the mall is open."

And then it hits — the realization that the mall will indeed be open tomorrow. Yes, the doors will open early, welcoming a special breed of shopper who is brave enough to risk being elbowed and shoved and maybe even stepped on in order to get the bargain of the ages. After all, there is no sale like an after-Christmas sale, and if we're really organized, we can buy next year's Christmas presents now and get them all for half-price!

Do you see what is happening in this scenario? The sun hasn't even set on Christmas Day, and already we are making plans and turning our thoughts back to the future.

Of course, not everyone rushes to the mall on December 26. Some people are more practical than that. They are the ones who do the laundry so that everyone will have something to wear to school or to work. Now that the church services and programs have concluded, they return the donkey costume or the angel outfit to the place where they rented it. If they do not have to return to work themselves, they go grocery shopping so that everyone will be well fed during the New Year's holiday. They put gas in the car and maybe even have an oil change. The super-strategic people go to Hallmark and buy birthday cards for the next twelve months and put them in a little file. Sometimes they even go ahead and put stamps on the envelopes! Whatever the activity, it is probably geared toward getting on with life or making plans for tomorrow — in other words, getting back to the future.

Far be it from me to discourage you from the after-Christmas sale of the century or from an oil change, but I would like to distract you just long enough to ask you to think beyond it and consider another important matter. In fact, I believe the importance of this issue far outweighs any fabulous deal you might find in the retail universe. I am talking about your life. Let's shift out of the material world for a moment and think about getting back to your future.

This season is full of gifts, and I hope you received some really wonderful presents from some really wonderful people. I think, though, that the greatest gift that comes along every year during the holiday season is the opportunity for a new beginning. Christmas begins the last week of the year, and in the week between Christmas and New Year's Day we have the chance to finish old business and "balance the books" in our lives. Then, when the clock strikes midnight on December 31, we are launched not only into a brand-new day but a brand-new year. It's a gift full of promise and potential, but like any other gift, it must be received and unwrapped and utilized.

Everyone has a chance to begin again, but not everyone takes it. Maybe you have not always availed yourself of the occasion to begin again. Maybe life has been difficult and you have been so discouraged in the past that you have even dreaded the new year. Or maybe you knew a new year would bring inevitable changes — a child leaving home to attend college or a retirement that you're not quite ready for — and you just didn't want to face it. Regardless of your situation, the chance for a new beginning awaits you, and you will need to decide whether or not you're going to take it.

During this holiday season, as we celebrate the birth of Jesus, we should remember that His birth symbolizes new beginnings, and He is the one who makes all things new. By the power of the Holy Spirit, He is constantly breathing new life into what was thought to be dead. He is bringing new hope to the most desperate situations. He is taking people who find themselves at the end of one journey and setting their feet on bright new paths of peace and joy and victory. He is drying tears and calming fears and injecting fresh courage into anxious souls.

He is the Star that we follow. But of course, you know that by now. He never leads us backwards, only forward. He can heal the past and remove the sting of the string of memories that stretch back through our lives. But He will not allow us to stop there. He is very busy, and He has a very special plan, a destiny, for you. He wants you to join Him and to reach your full potential as you participate in all that He has for you. You simply cannot do it unless you face forward and put one foot in front of the other and walk into the future.

I say to you that with every new beginning comes a chance to dream again. I am counting on you to have read the previous chapter of this book by now and to be well on your way toward letting go of your past and burying it, along with its pain, so deeply that it cannot ever influence you again. And now that you have done that, *dream*. Get back to your future and begin to think about what you want to see happen in the coming year in your life.

What do you want to see two years from now, or five, or ten? What passions do you want to pursue? What goals do you want to reach in your job or with your family or in your financial situation? Perhaps you would like to take a vacation or buy a house or pay off your debts. Perhaps you want to pass the bar exam or start your own business or learn to needlepoint. Maybe you want to complete a marathon or take a ride in a hot air balloon or lose a certain number of pounds. You may wish you could arrange your work schedule in such a way that you can spend more time with your family, because, after all, the children are only young once and you see how quickly they are growing up before your very eyes.

I cannot tell you what your dreams are. No, only you can do that. Only you know what excites you the way an after-Christmas sale excites a shopaholic. Only you know what causes your heart to leap when you begin to think about it. Only you can feel those unmistakable stirrings deep within you when you begin to ask yourself, "What if I could . . . ?"

Would you be willing to start to dream again right now? Would you be willing to let your thoughts run wild for a few minutes

and ponder the things you'd really like t
or experience? Would you be willir
complete the question, "What if 1
could . . . ?"

May I offer some advice as you begin to
dream again? On your journey back to the
future, let your thoughts wander as far
ahead as they can go and let your mind's eye
gaze as far as it can see. Dream big dreams;
dream God-sized dreams. But in your
dreaming, include a few dreams that can be
fulfilled in a reasonable amount of time and
some that will allow you to chart your prog-
ress toward them. Nothing will help you
keep dreaming like the joy of seeing some
come true.

A new year is on its way. Twelve months,
fifty-two weeks, three hundred sixty-five
days — and they're all yours. Let your
dreams live again, embrace the time to
come, and get yourself back to the future.

18

'Tis the Season

I hope you've figured out by now that I really do enjoy Christmas. We celebrate it with gusto at our house, and I like to be right in the middle of all the activity. I take over the kitchen, while my wife makes sure that the house is decorated inside and out, from top to bottom. But there's one part of the holiday I despise. No matter how hard I try to get myself out of it, I cannot avoid it; I cannot escape it; I cannot hide from it. I'm sure it happens at your house, too, but we'd have a hard time finding anybody on planet earth who absolutely hates it as much as I do.

Have you guessed yet what this despicable task is? It's the after-Christmas cleanup. Honestly, I would rather have a root canal than pull ornaments off the tree and wrap them in tissue paper and put them in a box. I would rather go ice skating in a pair of wet long johns than have to take down all the lights my wife puts up. I do not like to find a place for all that wrapping paper we didn't use, and I do not like putting those things called "knickknacks" back in their boxes until next December. Boycotts don't work; sit-ins don't convince her; even my deeply spiritual look and expressions of a need to lie before God for a message don't help me escape this duty (and that one normally is effective!).

Every year, I do my best to stretch my duties in the kitchen to the breaking point. I work so hard wrapping the leftovers, because that does take some time and energy, and I hope my wife will notice how much effort I expend. Once the leftovers are properly put away, I think of something to make with them — like, say, turkey soup. It's not that I really enjoy cooking leftovers; it's that I will do almost anything to get out of taking down the Christmas decorations.

"What's the big deal?" you ask. Okay, I might as well admit it: You see, because I am the man of the house, I am the one everybody looks to when someone needs to climb on the roof to deal with the lights outside, and I am afraid of heights. I do much better with both feet on the ground. I begin to get nervous just seeing a ladder.

Putting the lights on the house is considerably easier than taking them down. When I put them on, my wife is so excited. I climb down that ladder to a hero's welcome, with my heart expanded to the point I think it might burst because I have so delighted the woman I love. But the situation changes when the time comes to remove those lights. I am no longer the hero; I am just the handyman! The longer I put it off, the less of a hero I become. Inevitably, I begin to sense the pressure from the family. I know what they are thinking: *When in the world is Dad going to take those lights down?* Because I do know that there is an unspoken time limit on how long lights should stay up, I always give in and ascend the shaky ladder, one tentative rung at a time, reciting the Lord's Prayer and humming (or more aptly, chanting) "King Jesus Is A-Listening When You Pray" until I reach the summit of our home. Once there, I try not to look down because — well, that makes my head spin. (I never did believe in Santa Claus. Maybe, subconsciously, I knew no one in his right mind would spend so much time in the middle of winter on snow-covered roofs unless he had fallen into a jug of spiked eggnog!)

Once the daunting job of removing the lights has been completed, I expect to be able to sit down and enjoy a steaming cup of hot chocolate. In fact, conquering the roof, in my mind, should warrant a cup of hot chocolate with marshmallows. But do you know something? Everyone acts as though my feat is nothing more than a line item on the household "to-do" list. No one seems to understand what a big "to do" it is, and the next thing I know, I am sitting on the floor with a ceramic angel figurine in one hand and a fistful of Styrofoam peanuts in the other!

Christmas decorations celebrate and represent a specific time of year and they point to a particularly meaningful event — the birth of Jesus. When we hang wreaths on the door, ornaments on the tree, lights on the house, and stockings by the chimney with care, we are simply acknowledging that we are in the midst of a season that is different from any other time of the year, and that it is important to us. The accessories that adorn our house are special because they are seasonal.

How do you know when the Christmas season is coming? Do you simply take a peek at your calendar and count the weeks? Do you begin to get party invitations? Does it hit you when you hear the first notes of a Christmas song while you are out shopping or when you see those first red and green decorations in your favorite department store? Do you have some sort of internal mechanism that kicks into Christmas gear once Thanksgiving has passed? Is it the fact that pine trees and fir trees have taken over that once-empty parking lot and turned it into a small-scale industry? What is it that announces to you, most unmistakably, that Christmas is just around the corner?

The Bible says that the sons of Issachar were wise, for they had understanding of the times (1 Chronicles 12:32). How important it is to know the times, purposes, and seasons of your life! Knowing when to hold, when to fold, when to pack up, and when to move on is critical — not only concerning Christmas lights but far more importantly, in your life! Why leave up the decorations for a season in your life that is over? I believe that, for many of you, it is time to put away some things from your past and usher in a brand-new and provocative season. Now get up that ladder and take down those old lights, old attitudes, that old unforgiveness, and anything else that would cause you not to be ready for the new season that is coming to you in the new year!

One of the things that helped me survive so many changes in life was knowing when a season had ended and finding the grace to move on, even when it meant packing up some things and moving out of old places in my life. Something will signal a change of season to you from time to time, though it may not be as blatant as hearing Christmas music blasting over a public-address system at the mall. Your change-of-season sign may be as difficult as a layoff or the loss of someone you love; or it may be as thrilling as a marriage proposal, a new baby, or an unexpected promotion and a pay increase at work. It may also come as a sense of restlessness inside of you, a "knowing" that something needs to change, or the feeling that you have outgrown a job or a responsibility that once challenged you.

God made us this way. As we follow the Star, He leads us from one season to another, then on to another, for as long as we live. Season changes are some of the greatest growth opportunities we ever encounter, and they are designed to keep moving us farther along in His grand plans for our lives. Each season has unique beauties and special challenges; each one has a special purpose of preparation that may not be evident for months or years. But, one way we master the art of living is to accurately perceive the seasons of life, understand how to walk wisely through them, and squeeze the maximum joy out of every moment.

We don't have much trouble with the seasons of life when we are very young. No, we clearly move from one season to another when, as infants, we become strong enough to hold our heads up. We move again when we learn to feed ourselves. We enter new seasons when we learn to walk, when we learn to talk, and when we are finally potty-trained! As we continue to grow, certain seasons have built-in boundaries, thanks in part to the graded school system. There are certain time frames within which we learn to read, learn our multiplication tables, and learn to write in cursive. Massive season change takes place when we obtain a driver's license and when we graduate from high school.

Once we reach adulthood, the changes are not so clear-cut. By then we have gained a bit of life experience and maturity and, if we walk with the Lord, we have probably learned a thing or two about the way He leads us. In fact, the only way to really grasp a change of seasons is to be connected to Him and committed to following where He leads. I mentioned earlier some of the life events that may signal a change of seasons to you, but I need to tell you that it is dangerous to wait on circumstances to change before you make a move that God has ordained. Sometimes you must hear His voice for yourself and trust Him to guide you into a new season when your life seems to be a bed of roses. This is why you must know Him intimately and allow Him to develop a sensitive internal radar in you. That way, you will know when He is on the move for you, and you will be able to cooperate with Him and enter the new season with grace.

May I give you some real-life, practical examples? Trying to get married during a God-ordained season of singleness is as silly as pulling out Christmas decorations on the Fourth of July! If you accurately perceive that season, you will embrace it as a time of preparation and you will savor its benefits until God shows you clearly that it is time to marry. Likewise, applying for a job as CEO of a Fortune 500 company is out-of-season if you have just graduated from college last week. Chances are, you will need some time to be prepared for that corner office, and if you can grasp the purpose and learn to leap over the obstacles in every season along the way, you will be better prepared than ever.

Be very prayerful as you follow the Star. Don't settle simply for the warm glow of His light on your path but talk to Him and listen to Him. Let Him lead you with a whisper as He nudges you out of the old seasons and into new ones. Not only do I wish you happy holidays this year, I wish you a series of magnificent and joyful seasons as you follow Him from one season to the next, unfolding for you a wonderful life. Oh, and if at all possible, make sure that the ladder you climb is the one to success and not the one with the icicles hanging off the rungs — that first step can be a lulu!

19

The Gift That Keeps on Giving

We don't know their names or where they came from. The Bible calls them "wise men from the East," and scholars give us reason to believe they traveled by starlight out of Africa all the way to Jerusalem and on to Bethlehem. On foot, it was a long journey, but the star in the sky compelled them to keep walking. They *had* to make it to the place where Jesus was. I doubt they even needed to encourage one another; I suspect the star in the sky was enough to beckon them toward their destination.

When they entered Jerusalem, they accidentally stirred up trouble. In their eagerness to get to Jesus, they began to ask the local residents, "Where is He who has been born King of the Jews? For we have seen His star in the East and have come to worship Him" (Matthew 2:2). Now if you were a good law-abiding citizen of Israel, you might have been alarmed by such a question. After all, the Jews already had a king. Sure they did; his name was Herod and he lived in the palace down the street. If you were the king, you would feel further threatened — having had no notice that you were being replaced — and you might be especially bothered by that word "worship."

Being a diligent king and eager to protect his rightful throne, Herod began to investigate. He called his chief priests and scribes to find out what they knew about the so-called king. These men knew their scriptures, so they quoted an Old Testament prophet named Micah, who had written that the ruler of Israel would someday be born in the little town of Bethlehem. Still curious, but not wanting to attribute too much legitimacy to the wise men, he also sent for them secretly and asked them exactly what time the unusual star had appeared in the night sky. They told him; they didn't know any better. I guess they were so pure-hearted that it never occurred to them that anyone would want to harm the royal baby.

Herod was a master manipulator. He tried to make them feel important by giving them a job to do: "Go and search carefully for the young Child," he instructed, "and when you have found Him, bring back word to me, that I may come and worship Him also" (Matthew 2:8). Fully understanding their orders from the king, they set out again on their journey. I don't know whether they had a map or not; I don't know whether the road to Bethlehem was well-marked. All I know is that the star, which had led them to Jerusalem, began to lead them once more. And it didn't stop shining its light on their path until they arrived at their desired destination.

When they laid eyes on the infant King, those dignified wise men fell flat on their faces and began to worship Jesus. How could they have stayed standing in the presence of such majesty, such glory, such goodness? I understand that response, and perhaps you do too. Sometimes we just can't stand in the power of His presence, and when we get to the place where Jesus is, nothing else seems appropriate or even physically possible. He's just that awesome.

Once the wise men (who, by the way, had demonstrated their wisdom with their worship) were able to get back on their feet, they presented their treasures to Jesus. Oh, and what exquisite gifts they were! Gold and frankincense and myrrh. There is no telling what those presents were worth!

Now you know as well as I do that when a person is on the way to meet a king, he or she takes the best gift they can find. It might even be a gift that blows all of this month's budget and next month's too. Maybe sometimes the intent is to try and impress his Highness, but sometimes, too, a person just wants to give a gift that befits the power and the influence and the greatness of the king and to express honor for his position of supreme authority.

Let's give the wise men the benefit of the doubt. I, for one, believe they grasped the history-making moment in which they played supporting roles. I think they knew that Jesus was indeed a king like none who had ever sat — or would ever sit — upon an earthly throne. I think they gave Him the finest gifts money could buy, goods of the highest value. But I wonder if they really understood the Gift to whom they gave the gold, the frankincense, the myrrh. Did they know that their treasures paled in comparison to the treasure that Jesus is? Compared to the worth of Jesus, even the purest gold is like aluminum foil, frankincense is no better than a dollar-store candle, and myrrh no more valuable than petroleum jelly.

You see, Jesus was not a Gift for the short term. He did not make a one-time appearance on earth, live and minister for thirty-three years, and then return to heaven to watch what happens to the human race. No,

Jesus is the Gift for all time. By His Holy Spirit, He continues to live among us today. He is still doing what He did when He visited this world in the flesh. What do I mean by that? I mean that He is still healing the sick. He is still opening blind eyes. He is still setting free captive and tormented souls. He is still declaring liberty to all who are in bondage to addiction or depression or anxiety or anything else that keeps a person from living in the health and joy that He purchased for us on the Cross. He is still restoring what you thought was lost forever. He is still resurrecting dreams and directing destinies. He is still teaching men and women how to love one another and how to live overcoming lives. He is still pronouncing peace to the storms that ravage your daily existence. And He is still speaking the words of life. Over and over and over again, words of hope and healing and courage and victory are rolling off His lips, and they are making a beeline for you.

Jesus never runs out. He is our source, and the well of His life never runs dry. He is never empty, He's always full. You will never be able to drain Him or take all that He has. Have you been so rejected that you don't think there is enough love in the world to heal your hurting heart? Jesus has more than enough love. Have you been so disappointed that you are quite sure there is not enough hope in the world to lift you from despair? Jesus has more than enough hope. Have circumstances beyond your control thrust you into such grief that you honestly do not believe you will ever smile again? Jesus has more than enough joy to put that beautiful smile back on your face and to cause laughter to bubble up out of your belly again! He always has exactly what you need, and He always has more than enough. He is the Gift that keeps on giving. And He is the Star that I follow.

Jesus is the Star that outshines everything this world has to offer. He is the only One who can light your way and lead you safely down the sometimes treacherous path called life. He is the only One who can take your hand and bid you follow Him into the fulfillment of your God-given purpose. He is the only One who knows the grand destination that is your divine destiny — and the steps you need to take in order to get there. He is the only One who can place a dream in your heart and then cause it to come to pass in a way that will leave you grinning and shaking your head in total amazement. He is the only One you can really trust, and the only One worth trusting.

Would you go back with me for a moment to the wise men? Do you remember what happened to them after they fell down in worship and after they laid gifts before the young King Jesus? The Bible says that they were divinely warned in a dream not to return to Herod but to travel back to their own country along another route. The light of the star that led them to Jesus did not illuminate their path home. How could it? By that time they had already beheld the real Star. That other light in the sky really didn't matter anymore. They had seen the face of God — and then they could hear the voice of God guiding them, even as they slept, and giving them instructions for safe passage on their journey.

As it was for the wise men, so it is for all of us who have caught even the slightest glimpse of Jesus. Whether He has been burning brightly in your heart for years or whether you have just become acquainted with Him through this book, there is nothing I want more this Christmas than for you to follow the Star.

20

The Gift Remains

The ornaments are packed away, the Christmas leftovers have been eaten, and even the holiday music has ceased and been replaced with nonseasonal tunes. Relatives have returned from whence they came, and perhaps even the thank-you notes have already been mailed. Trash bags full of wadded-up wrapping paper and ribbon are awaiting their transport to the city dump. Those little tins that held all sorts of gifts and goodies have been emptied and stacked on the shelf to be recycled next year. And thank goodness, the lights that illuminated the house are rolled neatly on their spools, and I have safely ascended and descended the ladder to declare victory over the rooftop once again.

We had to rearrange furniture to make space for the tree when we brought it in, but now the room looks bare without it — and its grand boughs look so pitiful lying beside the mailbox. All over the house, there are places that seem naked because the decorations have been put away. I don't worry, though, because I know that this year, as with every year, our eyes will adjust, and within a week or so we will not even remember how beautifully bedecked the house was for Christmas. We will be back to normal, and everything will look just fine to us.

I suppose most households go through exactly what we do. Some people feel post-Christmas letdown, while others are so glad it's finally over. However you feel about it, the season does end, and the truth of the matter is that time marches on, demanding that life resume its regular routine. Adults face the culture shock of returning to the office after a few precious days off; someone has to pay the bills and pick up the dry cleaning and keep the pantry stocked. Children go back to school, and there are ball games and ballet lessons and birthday parties to think about, now that Christmas is over.

When all is said and done and sung and celebrated, what is left of this happening called Christmas? Oh, of course we have the presents — the new sweaters we will wear throughout the winter, the new gadgets we will use until they break or something else renders them obsolete, and the new jewelry that will sparkle on our fingers or our wrists for years to come. We have photographs and memories and a few Christmas cards that might be worth saving, but what can we really take away in our hearts? What difference does Christmas really make, and why is it special in the lives of believers?

Do you know what sets apart this wintertime holiday for us? It is the fact that our Gift remains. Jesus is not only the Star that we follow. He is the Gift of Christmas. He is the One we celebrate in the midst of the greenery and tinsel. But unlike all the trimmings of the season, He stays. He makes Christmas a perpetual season, and even though He does receive some special attention toward the end of the year, He is as present in the middle of August and at the beginning of March as He is during that last week of December.

There is something comfortable and easy about getting back to normal, but I always find myself hoping that we can carry a bit of Christmas into our normalcy. I want our ordinary days to be different *because* we have focused on Jesus for a season. Then again, nothing is normal or ordinary at all when Jesus fills our lives. He makes every day extraordinary and every experience special in its own wonderful way.

Sometimes, amid the busyness of a season like Christmas, it helps to be reminded of the Gift and of all that has been given to us in Him. Sometimes, we see so many pictures of Him lying in that manger that we could almost forget He is now sitting at the right hand of God making fervent intercession for us and dedicating Himself to our highest good. Sometimes, in the face of housecleaning and cooking, shopping and wrapping, we lose sight of the wonder and the simplicity of the Gift that is constantly, quietly making His home in our hearts, day after stressful day.

May I remind you that He is the Peace-giver. He is the One who tosses a blanket of calm over the chaos of life in this world and speaks to our personal storms: "Peace. Be still." He is the source of joy, for it bubbles out of Him like a fountain, and all we need to do is draw near and drink deeply. He is the One who brings strength and stability to uncertain times and the One who enables us to maintain our emotional equilibrium when we are surrounded by turmoil. He is the One who tenderly sweeps up the pieces of a shattered heart and puts them back together again. He is the One who gives us the ability to forgive the most heinous offenses and keep living in victory after we have been terribly wronged. He is the One who looks upon the daunting challenges that threaten us and says: "Fear not." He is the One who erases our sins and gives us a clean slate every time we ask. He knows every curveball life will throw and gives us the power to knock it out of the park.

My friend, this is the Gift who lives inside of us. He does not spend eleven months of the year in a box on a shelf in the attic. He takes up residence inside of us, and His transforming power changes everything about us. I don't believe He desires to be on display once a year but that His passion is to go about His business of healing and restoring and renewing us without ceasing. He does so much more than guarantee us a place in heaven after we have slipped through earth's grasp: He makes this life exciting and fulfilling as we allow Him to express Himself through us.

We honor the Gift at Christmastime, but throughout the year His fire keeps burning in our hearts, because He never goes away. We live in the presence of the Gift, and the Gift lives within us — the very life of God pulsing through our veins. I am not talking about walking around in a choir robe or beginning every sentence with "Praise God" or "Thus saith the Lord," nor am I referring to singing a solo in church or standing in worship with your hands upraised. I do not mean sitting in public with your hands folded and your head bowed, nor serving plates for two hours in a soup kitchen. Now, none of these activities is inherently bad, but they are not inherently good either. They are only graced with goodness when they spring from the heart.

You see, I am talking about letting the Gift that is within us flow through us so that being so full of the presence of Jesus He just spills over into our everyday thoughts and actions. I believe the Gift is at its best when we go about our daily lives in a way that is perfectly natural and purely practical but extremely spiritual at the same time. That happens when we motion for the lady with nothing but a loaf of bread to check out ahead of us at the supermarket, especially when we have enough groceries to fill the basket and that space underneath as well! It happens when the hairdresser makes a mistake on a color job and we choose to bless instead of curse her. It happens when we speak a kind word to the clerk at the driver's license office — the one who looks like the job is driving her up the wall. It happens when we take time out of our busy schedules to help a teenager understand the consequences of unhealthy choices and point him in the direction of wisdom. It happens when we look lovingly into the eyes of our spouse and offer a kiss on the cheek instead of yet another request to take out the trash. It happens when we refuse to judge someone, when we hold our tongue and when we decide to be patient just a few minutes more.

I do not know the specifics of your life, but you do. I suspect you know the people in your family or neighborhood or circle of acquaintances who have never received the Gift. You know the situations that are devoid of grace and the circumstances that need the truth of God injected into them. You know those hopeless areas that can only be changed when His power is brought to bear on them.

As your life returns to normal when the Christmas season has ended, I encourage you to take the Gift wherever you go. Oh, how I hope you will continue to unwrap His wonder in your everyday life and show Him off to those around you. You know, the world needs the Gift that you have, and in your own unique way, you can bring a little Christmas into every day.

About the Author

Bishop T. D. Jakes is the author of several books, including the *New York Times* bestsellers *God's Leading Lady*; *The Lady, Her Lover, and Her Lord*; and *Maximize the Moment*. His daily morning show, *The Potter's Touch*, and weekly broadcast, *The Potter's House*, air on Trinity Broadcasting Network and Black Entertainment Television in the United States, and in Europe and South America. Bishop Jakes is the founder and pastor of Potter's House, one of the fastest-growing churches in the nation, where he pastors an interracial congregation of more than 26,000 members. He lives in Dallas with his wife and their five children.